CAREERS IN COMEDY

CAREERS IN COMEDY

By

SHARON MENZEL-GERRIE

The Rosen Publishing Group, Inc.
NEW YORK

Published in 1994 by The Rosen Publishing Group, Inc.
29 East 21st Street, New York, NY 10010

First Edition

Menzel-Gerrie, Sharon.
  Careers in comedy / Sharon Menzel-Gerrie.
    p.   cm.
  Includes bibliographical references and index.
  ISBN 0-8239-1517-4   ISBN 0-8239-1713-4 (pbk.)
    1. Stand-up comedy—Vocational guidance—Juvenile
literature. [1. Stand-up comedy—Vocational guidance.
2. Vocational guidance.] I. Title.
  PN1969.C65M46   1993
  792.7'028'023—dc20   93-4962
                                                                   CIP
                                                                    AC

Cover photo: Dave Chappelle at the Boston Comedy Club, New York City. Dave began his career in Washington, D.C., and now splits his time between New York City and Los Angeles. At the time this book was published, this nineteen-year-old phenomenon had been featured in two movies, two TV pilots, and sixteen national television shows.

Peter Berberian photo.

All photographs, except those of Dee Macaluso, David Daniel, Ron Crick, and Sharon Menzel-gerrie, are by courtesy of AP/Wide World Photos.

Manufactured in the United States of America

Dedicated to my heroes

About the Author

Sharon Gerrie grew up in a small town in Iowa whose claim to fame theretofore had been as the home town of Jean Seaberg and Lennox Industries (and no, she never met her or "Atta Boy" Dave). After college she joined Dudley Riggs's Brave New Workshop, an improvisational comedy revue company in Minneapolis, as an actress. There she met and married Paul Menzel. In 1977 Paul and Sharon moved to Houston and opened The Comedy Workshop as a cabaret theater for improvisation. Two years later The Comix Annex, a 90-seat hole-in-the-wall nightclub, opened, and comedy in Texas was born. The Comix Annex was the first and remained the strongest developmental nightclub for stand-up comedians in the Southwest until it closed in January 1990. In 1980, "just to keep the comics from taking my phone apart every day," Sharon started a booking agency for stand-up comedians (and variety artists). Maintaining the agency allowed Sharon to see what must be by now hundreds of comedians. "This book was written in self-defense. I ran out of time and patience telling young comics all these things; so I decided to write them all down."

Professionally, Sharon is a veteran of seven-shows-a-week comedy revues, Houston radio and TV commercials, industrial and feature films, and Houston-based musical theater. She currently runs and maintains a booking agency for stand-up comedians and does free-lance public relations for local arts groups. Sharon lives (when she finally gets home) outside Houston with second husband Andy, teenage son Andrew, two cats (Gus and Jack) and her beloved computer ("Isn't spell-check the coolest thing?"). Sharon would like to be a writer when she grows up.

Contents

Preface

In 1979, The Comedy Workshop in Houston, Texas, an established venue for improvisational revues, opened The Comix Annex, a ninety-seat room for stand-up comedians. The Comix Annex was the first stand-up comedy club in Texas and, until it closed in 1990, one of the best developmental rooms in the country. The room was good because the standards were high. Stage time was difficult to come by. Competition was fierce, and the " . . . but my friends all think I'm funny" people soon went back to their day jobs. A year after the Annex opened, a booking agency for comedy talent and variety artists was started. Shortly after that I became booking agent for The Comedy Workshop. I had extensive experience as a performer and as a club owner, but none as a booking agent for comics. Fortunately, I learned *my* part of the business quickly and in doing so learned many of the dos and don'ts of the business side of *your* job—that of stand-up comedian.

When the Annex opened, it was intended to be a training ground for the comedy stars of tomorrow. That goal was accomplished: The alumni list is impressive. It is thrilling to watch the comics who started on the Annex stage take career steps up. One and all, they are comedians of exceptional abilities.

It takes a long time and a lot of work to be a big name in this business. However, you can start being a professional the first time you pick up a microphone. Over

Bill Cosby at an opening night performance at New York City's Radio City Music Hall.

the years, countless young comics have asked me about topics that are covered in this book. What you are about to read reflects my personal opinion based on experience and discussions with other agents, managers, bookers, and club owners. Not everything is gospel, but if you try my suggestions at least you won't shoot yourself in the foot.

1

The World of Funny Business

You're sitting at home. The TV is on, and you're flicking through the cable channels. A few old sit-coms, a couple of movies, sports, weather, and station after station of comedy. "Comedy Central," "Night at the Improv," "Ladies of the Night," Showtime's comedy this and HBO's comedy that. Comedy (and comedians) everywhere. You see comedians hosting talk shows, acting in sit-coms—network and cable, selling products in commercials, and doing lots and lots of stand-up comedy. You watch the comics night after week after year. Some you laugh at and some you don't. But whether you laugh at them or not, you begin to notice that these people have what appears to be a great job. In fact, these are people with one hell of a job! You start to take a look at this comedy thing as a career choice.

You look closer. There are comedy clubs all over the country, so comedians must go from club to club every week of the year. That means they get to travel all the time, see the country—which is fun. If they're traveling, they're probably living in nice hotels every week, which means you wouldn't have to worry about

1

keeping up a permanent address—which means no rent costs. In fact, all you probably have to do is hire an answering service to take your phone messages—all you'd need in the way of roots. All comics wear cool clothes. That has to mean that it's pretty easy to pull in big bucks. Comics always seem young and to hang out with movie stars or famous people—meaning that making it big, fast, must be no problem. And—best of all—comedians barely have to work. They are only on stage or in front of the camera for half an hour or so each day, and then it's quitting time. All they have to do is think up a few jokes, and it's easy street. What a life! Yes, let's definitely consider comedy as a career.

You walk over to the mirror and take a good, hard look. Young, with your whole life ahead of you—that's a plus. Fairly good-looking, good personality, great at parties—everyone always laughs at your jokes and in school you were the class clown. All that has *got* to mean you're funny. The comics you see on TV are all pretty young too, which means they probably started doing comedy right out of high school. It also means they didn't have to put in four years of college. In fact, because they're all so different, you probably don't need much formal training at all to be a stand-up. All that really could be a little hard is to come up with a routine. And get established in one of the comedy clubs. And get some work lined up. But, when it comes down to it, how hard can that be? You write a couple of jokes and fill out your time with funny stuff you've heard others say here and there. No problem. You make a few calls to the local comedy clubs and let them know you are going to come in and do a few jokes for them. They will probably be really impressed that the next comedy superstar is going to drop by.

Yes, sir, this comedy thing is starting to take shape. This is a chance to break out of the mold and do something different with your life. You decide to give it a shot. You sit down and start to make plans. You'll write a killer routine this afternoon, practice it for a while, and then quit your job or school. You'll scrap your plans for college (I mean, who needs to waste four years and all that money) and be a stand-up comedian. In fact, if you work really hard, you could probably start pulling in good money in a couple of weeks. So you sit down, pen in hand, and start to write. After half an hour you don't have much written. It's not that you can't think of funny stuff; you can. It's just that by the time you get it written down, it doesn't seem funny anymore. Maybe what you should do is call the nearest comedy club and tell them you are coming over tonight to perform. That will put the pressure on you to write, and you always work better when you are under the gun.

Time out. If what you have read so far sounds vaguely familiar, read on. Read on before you make the call to quit your job or drop your school plans and dive feet first into the world of comedy. Comedy club owners and booking agents routinely get calls from people who want to know in five minutes or less what it takes to make it big in comedy. They're in a hurry. Time's a-wasting. If they are told that the road to stardom is not what it seems, they counter that this time things will be different. They are sure that in their case standards do not apply. They are unique, special, the exception to the rule. They are *really* funny. All those others who have said the same thing are just kidding themselves. You'd be blown away if you could see this act.

These are eager, well-meaning folks who see stand-up comedy as a way to become famous and make fast money. They watch comics on TV and in the clubs, and the whole process seems so easy, so smooth. They see no reason why they can't fit into the comedy world as easily and with as much splash as the stand-ups they see on TV. All they really need is one good break . . .

Well, first off, they're right. There isn't a reason in the world why a young person can't make it in comedy today. The marketplace is huge and diversified. There will always be room for one more incredible talent, or gifted writer, or unique personality. Unfortunately, the problem hinges on the fact that not everyone who would like a career in comedy falls into one or more of those three categories. And there are lots and lots of people who would like to have a career in comedy. In any comedy club with an amateur night, dozens of would-be comedians compete each week for the few performing slots available. It is more likely that the new person will be put on a waiting list for an amateur night slot than "go up" the first time. The wait may be as long as several weeks.

The person who keeps coworkers in stitches or is the class clown must remember that these are informal, contained situations in which the "audience" has lots in common with the "comic." The laughter the "comic" hears is not so much at the "joke" as at the inside knowledge that the "audience" shares with the teller. So the joke about the teacher who wears a toupee and thinks his secret is safe will be much less effective in front of a comedy club audience than with the students or coworkers who watch his daily struggle to keep his rug on straight. Comedy clubs, TV audiences, and concert audiences are groups of strangers without these common bonds to the comic or the subject matter. The task of the stand-up comedian is writing material that will appeal to a large section of the populace in general. It requires looking at the subject from an entirely different slant than some other comedian and being funny at the same time.

And, because the marketplace *has* become so huge

and diversified, stand-up comics today have to do everything they can to separate themselves from the pack. This difference can manifest itself in the way the comedian looks or acts physically. Usually it manifests itself in the type of material the comedian writes. Comedians cannot simply "write a couple of jokes and fill out their time with funny stuff they've heard here and there." First, they can't afford to use another's routine. That is considered stealing in the comedy business. True, the comedy police won't come knocking on your door and arrest you for joke theft; but stealing material is a good way to stop in this business before you begin. It is considered unethical; it always comes back to haunt and embarrass the thief, and it definitely will not help you build a positive reputation with club owners or other comics. Second, using material that is identifiable with another person lessens rather than increases the popularity and unique identity of the borrower. Third, audiences stop laughing at things they have heard over and over again. With all the stand-up comedy available on a daily basis, audiences have become well educated to what they like and don't like. This author was once watching audition tapes. Three, count them, three comics started their routines with the exact same joke. As it was impossible to tell who was the legitimate author (it is quite possible that none of them was), and because the thing did not get funnier in the telling, no one got a job. Comedy club owners and booking agents like to think that each week they are hiring different kinds of comedians for their stage. Variety insures them the repeat business they need from a local audience. If audiences fail to get variety and attendance drops, have no doubt that the owner will quickly weed out the clones and continue on with business.

So the world of comedy just got a little more complicated! What you have read does not mean that you are not a funny person or that you cannot write funny material. It simply means that building your routine will not happen overnight and that your first attempts at comedy writing will, it is hoped, not be as good as the material you write two years from now. Any professional writer will tell you that nothing is written once and that's it: You write and rewrite and then rewrite a little more. Stand-up comedy material is no different. Writing solid, quality comedy material takes a lot of trial and error and the humility to separate yourself from the material and hear what the audience is telling you. Stories that crack your friends up but fall flat in front of several audiences obviously have some problems in the funny department. In short, becoming a working stand-up comedian takes time. Which brings us back to our eager young friend at the beginning of the chapter. This person expected to cancel college plans, quit the job in a month or so, and start living in the lap of luxury from stand-up comedy income. Once again, time out!

Stand-up comedy is show business. It's fun, exciting, and creative, but it never stops being a business. Like any other business, people who want to invest their lives in comedy need to train, develop, learn, and—carefully—grow. You are the raw material. Your routine or "act" is the product of the raw material. Like any manufacturer, you need financial backing, marketing, research, development, a popular product, and a good business plan. No matter how you slice it, getting this career off the ground takes as much time and effort as starting a new business. Stand-up comedy is a lot of things, but one of the things it is not is a short ride on the gravy train. The comedians you see on TV and cable and in the clubs do make it look easy. In reality, however, it can take even a very gifted comic years of hard work to get to the point where line after funny line rolls out like water off a duck's back. In reality, the comics you see on TV and cable have put in years of effort to be able to do those five minutes or so. In reality, some people who try for years and years to be stand-up comedians never make it beyond the local amateur night.

The bottom line in show business is that no one cares whether it took you five years or five minutes to come up with your act. If you and your material are funny and you are lucky enough to connect with an audience, you have a chance. If not, you don't. To think to yourself (or worse yet, to say to a club owner), "I've put in two years. I deserve to be hired—or given a better performing slot," is entirely the wrong approach. Show business is two parts luck, three parts timing, two parts stamina, and one part talent. There is no such thing as tenure. No one gets a gold watch at the end of twenty years.

Why do it, then? you ask. If there are thousands of young comics out there glutting the market, and it's going to take forever and a day to be discovered with no guarantees—why do it? Do it because (1) if you make it big every effort will have been worthwhile; (2) if you don't make it, you will still have had a wonderful adventure; (3) a cultivated sense of humor can be the voice of sanity in a violent and crime-ridden world; and (4) the skills you gain as a comedian, even in a short career, will always be of service to you.

You walk back over to the mirror and take another look. Now you're not quite sure what to do. Comedy looks interesting but definitely not as easy as it did a few pages ago. In fact, comedy is starting to look like a pretty hard way to make a name for yourself and some money. What to do? You're starting to feel discouraged.

Don't be discouraged. The intent of what you have read so far and what is to come is not to keep you out of this field. The intent is to give you reality-based

7

Mike Meyers (Wayne Campbell) and Dana Carvey (Garth) perform their popular skit "Wayne's World" on "Saturday Night Live."

information about a specific business. Show business can dazzle the novice. It can also leave that same person broke and bitter in a very short time. The information that follows is designed to give someone who has never been on stage as a stand-up comedian a no-frills explanation of what the craft requires. It may not always be what you want to hear, but better to read about the pitfalls than to experience them at great financial and emotional cost. After you have finished reading, you should be able to make an educated assessment of whether or not this comedy stuff is really for you. Read on.

2

Who Are Stand-Up Comics?

When you watch comedians, one of the first things you notice is how different they all are. Some are slow and deadpan; others are walking balls of energy. Some have silly, goofy, short jokes, others tell long anecdotes, and still others are almost intentionally esoteric. Some always wear a business suit and comment on topical events. Some wear a costume. Some play musical instruments as a part of their act, and others do magic tricks. Surely it would be impossible to come up with any kind of accurate personality profile.

Yes, it is difficult to stereotype comedians. Careers in this business are always in a state of flux. One may be up or down as a comic, but rarely in stasis. Some comics start out with one kind of act and evolve into another format during the progress of their career. An example might be a young comic who starts out doing straight stand-up comedy with no audiovisual aids. After a time the comic adds a guitar or a portable keyboard, making him or her a comic-musician rather than a straight stand-up comic. However, comics do share certain characteristics; let's look at the similarities.

PERSONALITY PROFILE

Most comics are extroverts. They enjoy being the center of attention. Many actually were the class clown. They enjoy the positive reinforcement that comes when they hear people laughing. They feel accepted. Many working comics say that there is nothing in the world like the feeling that comes when the audience laughs. Many established comics continue to do concerts and clubs simply for the stimulation they get from a live audience. That is not to say that comics don't get nervous before going on stage; they do. Many seasoned comedians routinely experience stage fright or butterflies in the stomach before they perform.

More to the point, most comics do not view public speaking as a negative as more introverted people tend to do. Something about standing alone in the spotlight with only a microphone attracts them like a moth to a flame. Stage or film actors often say that stand-up comedy looks scary even to them. The comic is "all alone out there." As a general rule, stand-up comics can't rely on sets or costumes or other actors. They are theatrically naked, going before an audience with only their material and wits about them. The extrovert in the comic loves crowds and is comfortable meeting new people. The person who is basically quiet, shy, self-contained, and a poor mingler will not find this profession appealing.

Another trait that comics seem to share is a belief in self that helps them focus on promoting themselves and their careers. They believe they are funny (often before anyone agrees with them). They believe they can make it to the top (often without any tangible evidence). They are one hundred percent convinced that comedy is the best of all possible choices for them (often without the agreement of family or friends—or audiences).

This amazing self-reliance promotes positive self-

11

esteem and self-motivation. One rarely hears comics say that they had a bad set or that their act was terrible. Evenings when their routine went over poorly bring a response such as "The audience was quiet," or "They had a little trouble out there," or "Tough crowd." What you are more likely to hear is, "I killed tonight!" or "My set was really hot."

Self-motivation in a comic is purely a survival instinct. Even beginning comedians soon figure out that no one is going to take them by the hand and lead them to stardom. They are on their own to succeed or fail. They must discipline themselves to write and continually improve their act. They know there will never be less competition; always more. Working comedians know that unless calls are made, the work won't be forthcoming. Working comedians know that materials like brochures and pictures must be kept in supply if they are to continue to break into new markets. They know that they must maintain healthful eating habits and exercise to keep their career on an upward spiral. The traditional nine-to-five, Monday-to-Friday workweek will not be there to provide structure; they must do it internally. Most comics live by a very strict regimen of their own design. At first, this structure is a means of focusing on their career, but eventually, if the comics are persistent and good, the discipline helps them attain some higher career goal such as securing the agent they want, or getting a screenplay seen, or going to the right film auditions. If you ask working comics why they always make their booking calls in the morning, or write every day between two and four, or play video games after shows instead of partying, they will tell you these are rituals they have carried out for years. The habits and attitudes you cultivate as a beginning comic stay with you for a long time. If you make thoughtful, healthy choices, your career will be served.

Another pair of personality traits that most comics have (and others would do well to adopt): the ability to blend into new circumstances quickly, and an easygoing attitude to life in general. If your goal as a beginning comedian is to make it big, it is a foregone conclusion that you will have to travel. Comedy clubs all over the country are a little bit the same and a little bit different; audiences, too. It is the wise comedian who can become acclimated to constantly new circumstances without a jolt to the nervous system. Attached to these comedy clubs are all kinds of variables in the form of people, places, and things. If you are the kind of person who likes everything in the same place, i's dotted and t's crossed, the life of a stand-up will not agree with you. If, on the other hand, you are a hang-loose person with the overall attitude of taking what comes and making the best of it, you may be a comic yet.

Another thing most comics have in common is good health. This is no accident. Many stand-ups are very careful about what they consume and are daily exercisers. The primary reason? Comics simply can't afford to be sick. If they are too sick to work, they do not get paid. Club owners cannot afford to pay two comics for the same job, even if one is unavoidably ill. Traveling takes comics through different parts of the country. They need to be healthy to ward off a virus going around in Chicago so as not to be sick in San Francisco the next week. People who need regular care from the same doctor will find the profession prohibitive. People who need regular medication have to plan their traveling carefully. People who need to stay relatively close to one area for health reasons will find their career limited. They will also find themselves frustrated. If you have a tendency to be sick a lot, you should reconsider a career in this field. The best regimen for the comic is to eat well, exercise, and get adequate sleep.

Stand-up comedy is a highly social profession. Comedy clubs have attached bars, and audiences come to party and be entertained. Comedians who start to drink, smoke, and use recreational drugs because "everyone in the club is doing it" will suffer physically. Smoking, drinking, and drug use impair the comedian and damage the career as they do other occupations. Excesses do not make you funnier. In fact, they are more than likely to have the opposite effect. On stage, some comedians make life on the road sound like one big social event. They talk about being constantly wined and dined and adored. They make everything sound glamorous. From the outside, they seem to live exotic and enviable lives. Don't be fooled. Comics have to get up in the morning, pay taxes, pick up the laundry, and put their pants on one leg at a time just like everyone else. What a comic says on stage doesn't have to be the truth—it just has to be funny. More on this later.

Let's review the personalty traits that comedians tend to share:

- Extroverted nature
- Positive attitude/high self-esteem
- Self-reliance
- Self-motivation
- Adaptability
- Good physical health

This is not to say that shy violets who are nervous in crowds, compulsive about their surroundings, and sickly cannot be funny. It just means that if you are more introverted you may be risking a difficult, un-happy life in a field that plays so far from your type. In this career, the single most important thing you can do for yourself is bounce back easily from setbacks. If each disappointment—and there will be some—sinks you further and further into depression, perhaps you should look for a career with more predictability.

EQUAL OPPORTUNITY

While we're on the subject of personalities, let's look at careers in comedy from an equal-opportunity point of view. Just from watching TV, it is evident that show business in general and comedy specifically employ a fairly even mix of talent racially. Some noticeable imbalances exist, however, under the general headings of age, physical ability, and gender.

As you observe comedians, one thing you will notice is that they all seem fairly young. It is rare to find a middle-aged to senior citizen looking comic in the clubs or on TV. Part of the reason you don't see a lot of silver hair and sagging was mentioned earlier: Comics who are on the road all the time tend to take good care of themselves physically. It's not that they never turn forty—they just don't look forty. The rest of the reason is that being a working comic takes a young person's energy and freedom from responsibilities. Working comics travel a great deal, live out of a suitcase, and for all intents and purposes have no real roots. As people get older, they tend to have homes and relationships and children that are difficult to leave week after week. After some time on the road, most comics start looking for ways to practice their craft without leaving home so often. Also, as comics grow in popularity, so does the amount per show they can charge. After a certain point, successful comedians do not have to work as hard or do as many shows per year to support their life-style. Some older comedians are currently working the circuits, but they are in the minority. They tend to bill themselves as novelties: "Comedy's grandmother" or "The silver fox of comedy."

Another minority in the comedy business are the

15

physically challenged. While a disability does not rule out a career in comedy, it is a definite hurdle in a rejection-prone industry. Traveling and all its concomitant problems for the disabled do not go away because one is a comedian. If the person needs the regular attention of a medical professional, road work will be prohibitive. Also, most stages in comedy clubs are not barrier-free. The actual clubs must meet accessibility requirements, but the stage need not. Again, there are comedians currently on the circuits with severe physical disabilities. They are very good, and many have arranged sponsorship of their act through organizations that fund research for their particular disorder. If any one group exemplifies the drive, dedication, and determination that it takes to be a stand-up comedian, it is the physically challenged comic. However, a disability makes this difficult life-style even harder.

Last, but certainly not least, is the issue of gender imbalance in the field. As you watch the comics in the clubs and on TV, you will notice that most of them are men. As an educated guess, there are probably six males to every female stand-up comedian in the business today. Why? Show business in general seems to be pretty evenly divided. Why so much discrepancy in the world of stand-up comedy?

Stand-up comedy as a performance art is at once very old and very young. The first stand-up comedians traveled with vaudeville and then burlesque shows. The comedian was traditionally the man who kept the audience occupied while scenery and costumes were being changed behind the curtain. Often they were not stand-ups in the modern sense, but sketch artists working with a (usually female) helper. The helper rarely spoke and more often than not was the butt of the joke. A few "monologists" or stand-ups worked alone telling funny stories; these were all male. Ironically, America's love of the comedian came about through radio rather than live performance. Traveling shows went into cities across the country, but radio went into every living room. Fred Allen, Charlie McCarthy and Edgar Bergen, Jack Benny, Burns and Allen—all were comedians in the sense that we know today. Their monologs or duo acts were not tied to a continuing story line as the serial comedy programs were. They generally told jokes or anecdotes based on current events or life observations just as today's comedians do. It should be noted that the men in this era largely played themselves. They were under no social pressure to assume a character to be funny. Their female counterparts (of which there were few) almost always assumed a stage persona. A good example was Gracie Allen. A smart business woman and talented actress, Gracie won success when she assumed the "dumb, dizzy blonde" stereotype against husband George Burns as straight man.

If one dissects a joke, its backbone gives some insight into why males rather than females traditionally were drawn to and accepted in the role of comedian. Humor is based on a strong opinion. It is assertive. The teller of the joke is an independent voice asking a group to laugh at what the teller thinks is absurd. Assertiveness and independence were not characteristic descriptions of women until the women's movement began to exert social impact in the 1960s. If a woman wanted to be a stand-up comic, she was more likely to create an act around a self-deprecatory persona. For example, the self-proclaimed first female stand-up comedienne, Phyllis Diller, found that dressing like a lady and telling jokes was getting her nowhere fast. In *Spare Ribs*,* she is quoted as saying, "People back then [1955] were not

---

* Collier, Denise, and Beckett, Kathleen (New York: St. Martin's Press, 1980).

17

ready for a lady comic. They had no basis for accep-
tance." It was only after she started wearing outrageous
clothing and tearing down herself, her husband, and
anything else she could think of that Phyllis Diller
gained recognition as a stand-up comic.

This type of female stand-up was the only version of
comedienne from the mid-1950s to the late 1960s, as
exemplified by the work of Joan Rivers and the late
Totie Fields. As the demand for comedians grew, so did
the number of women venturing into the craft. By the
late 1960s to mid-1970s the comediennes had largely
dropped the comic costumes in favor of street attire, but
many still centered their material on "women's issues."
The problem of attracting females to stand-up comedy
was still a societal one. Cracking jokes was considered
brash and unladylike. Young women in the '70s had
plenty of serious role models, but few in the world of
stand-up comedy. Even progressive homes that would
support a show business career would have frowned on
the life of a stand-up comic for a daughter. Going on the
road was viewed as a riskier proposition for young
women than for men. It was during this period that the
world was hearing a lot of "the first woman to . . .".
Ground-breaking was going on everywhere for women.

Another reason that women have come late to the
field is, frankly, the attitude of male comedians. Stand-
up comedy was like a locker room when it started to
gain national attention. The "guys" would do their sets
and then hang out together after the show. There was
no room for anyone who didn't fit the comic stereotype.
No jugglers, mimes, prop comics, magicians, or women
need apply. Anyone with other than a straight stand-up
act found himself on the outside looking in as far as
peer-group bonding was concerned.

Today the field is wide open for women (and other
variety artists). In fact, many booking agents go out of

their way to find a change of pace from the two or three all-men lineups. Life on the road is still as draining as it was a decade ago, but infinitely more predictable for both the club owner and the comic. Maintaining long-distance relationships is just as difficult for men as for women comics. And pay scales tend to vary with geographic area and place in the lineup rather than other criteria. In other words, the challenges involved in making a comedy career work today are just as consuming for the male comedian as the female. The difference between today's comediennes and the brave first few is that audiences have become used to seeing women be themselves and still be funny. Although a lot of "women's humor" is still done by female comedians, it is no longer expected that this sort of material is all an audience will accept from a woman. Funny is funny.

AN INTERVIEW WITH DEE MACALUSO

When you first meet Dee Macaluso the word "interesting" comes immediately to mind. Not young, but not old. Tallish, model-thin, not beautiful, not ugly. Big sad eyes and hair-color-of-the-month. Kind of shy and yet kind of brassy. You start eliminating what she isn't to put her in context. Not a banker type or a nurse type or a CPA or anything corporate. Then you talk to her for a while and you get this sense of being with a '90s version of Holly Golightly—an older and wiser version. She has this kind of duality about her. If Dee had a sign on her forehead that said: "I'm a fortyish mom, I do car pools, and temp work sometimes, volunteer for charity functions, and I drive a Mercedes," you'd lean back and say, "Yeah, I can see that." On the other hand if the sign read: "I'm a stand-up comedian, an actress, a writer, a singer, a dancer, a person who can get real laid-back at parties, and I drive a Harley," you'd lean back and say, "Yeah, I can see that too." And either

Dee Macaluso

sign you read would be true. Dee is, among other things, a stand-up comedian. After six-plus years as a comic, she works in the open and middle or feature slot. She has, by her own admission, about 90 solid minutes of material. Only 90 minutes? Doesn't that bother her? Her reply, "Naw, I'm a work in progress." That word "interesting" still comes to mind.

I caught up with Dee during a rehearsal. She was preparing to do the role of Adelaide in a production of *Guys and Dolls* at Houston's huge outdoor theater in Miller Park. Adelaide is usually played by women ten years younger, but the early rehearsals I saw indicated that age wouldn't be a problem for Dee. We sat at a little table in the lobby, and Dee talked comedy.

Q: Tell me about yourself . . . a little history.

A: Well . . . [she's composing] let's see. I grew up in Buffalo, New York. There were five kids in the family, three boys, a sister, and me. I went to Buffalo State and got a BA and got married and had two kids and started comedy in 1987 and my husband died last year and I have rehearsal today. That's it. Can I go?

Q: No. When did you first start doing comedy?

A: I got into comedy, and then I got into stand-up. In about 1986 or so I auditioned for The Comedy Workshop's revue company and got in. We would write the shows and perform them, and they were all comedy. After the set show we would do improvisations for the audience, and they were all comedy—at least that was the goal. Sometimes it felt like tragedy. Then after the show I would go next door to the Annex, the stand-up side of The Workshop, and watch the comics work out. It took me about a year of watching and telling myself

21

"I can do that" to get up the nerve to take the plunge. So that makes it about 1987, and I just started going up on amateur night and worked my way up the comedy ladder.

Q: What were you doing before that to make a living?

A: I was a public relations director for a YWCA and a creative writer for Goodwill—that sort of thing. Then I decided to pursue acting, so that meant very little money and lots of sales jobs (with flexible schedules). I was lucky that my husband had a good job and was real supportive of all my creative stuff. But once I started comedy, well, that kind of pulled everything together for me. It was the place where all the lines intersected. I can literally use every damn skill I've got as a stand-up: acting, writing, directing, costuming, accounting, marketing, sales, clerical, and ironing.

Q: Those are all your skills?

A: I have a few more, like power-tool proficiency, but my kids will probably read this and well, you need some secrets.

Q: Tell me about your kids.

A: I have two great kids. Two daughters. Both teenagers. Both interested in show business.

Q: Does it bother you to go on the road as a comic and leave them?

A: I guess it's always going worry you to leave your kids. But my girls are real strong and together. I trust them, and it's worked out. All they really need these days is a reliable driver. So when I go away, I get someone to stay with them who's willing to keep up with their schedules—and I call a lot. I have this line, "When you have a son you just worry about one penis. When you have daughters you worry about all of them." I use that in my act.

Q: What was the best night in stand-up comedy for you, so far?

A: Best night. It was really best nights. In Amarillo at a little club called Jolly's. It was a [full] week club, and I was the feature. That whole week was magic. I could *not* say anything unfunny. The crowds loved me every single night. During the day we went horseback riding and drove through the countryside, which is beautiful. When I'd go into a store in town, people would recognize me. It was what I imagine being a celebrity must be all about.

Q: What was the worst night in stand-up for you, so far?

A: No question. Buffalo. I can't remember, or I repressed, the name of the club. Anyway, Buffalo's my home town. I had a booking there, my family came out to see me, and I bombed. I couldn't get *smiles* even. The most sound that came from that audience was this kind of groan part way through. Then, if bombing wasn't its own reward, I had to go out and sit with my family through the rest of the show. They were really nice. Finally one of them said, "We like you anyway." I wanted the earth to swallow me up.

Q: Talk about being a female and a comedian. Is your road more difficult to travel as a female?

A: Well, if you're asking if I've ever gotten the cold shoulder from the Boy's Club, you're right. It was difficult being accepted by the other comics. Anyone who's been in the stand-up business for about two minutes knows that if you don't start out being (a) male and (b) someone who only does straight comedy,* you start off one down. The guys are fun and I like them as a group, but they begrudge giving up pieces of their craft to people who aren't just like them. Maybe it validates them to acknowledge only like qualities. But remember, I grew up with three brothers. Fitting in with the guys has always been a part of my life. Besides, it really wasn't that tough. It hurt sometimes to be excluded, but I got over it.

Q: Hurt? When?

A: Well, I remember this time at the Annex. This famous comic was there, and he was talking to a bunch of people about some movie. He was going on and on about how great this film was, and no one in the group had seen it. No one except me. He kept saying, "I can't believe you guys haven't seen this flick," and I HAD. I kept saying, "I saw it." "I saw it." He just kept on going like I was invisible. I knew him, he knew me, but my opinion wasn't important. I know this is a small incident, but when you lump them all together they start to get painful.

Q: Are you bothered by sexual harassment on the road?

A: Not nearly enough. I'm kidding, of course. Don't get that politically correct, pained look. It was a joke. This is about comedy. Actually, I know all kinds of stuff happens on the road. But I'm not a fearful person, and I refuse to live in fear of something that *might* happen. When I'm in a condo with a male comic we just

---

* "Straight" comedy in this context refers to a comic whose act is all material. The comic uses no audiovisual aids, no musical instruments, or magic in his or her act.

go our separate ways. I mean, I'm not fearful, but I'm not stupid either.

Q: Would you like it if one of your daughters became a stand-up?

A: That would be OK. They're both in show business anyway, and this is just one aspect of show business. I look at any work you do in this business as a phase in a process.

Q: What advice would you give young people starting out in comedy?

A: Watch a lot at first and develop your own style. That's so important. It singles you out from the pack. Don't even try to imitate people you admire. You don't want to be that really great comic with an act just like Jerry Seinfeld. You want to be Jerry Seinfeld. Go to a bunch of amateur nights and go up whenever you can. Amateur nights are great confidence-builders. No matter how bad you are, there is going to be someone worse and you'll feel better. Be fearless and believe in yourself.

Q: How do you write material? Where do the ideas come from?

A: I know some comics spend specific portions of the day writing. They approach it in a kind of regimented way. I like to talk about life and observations about people. I keep a journal with me all the time and if something strikes me as interesting I make a note about it and then flesh it out when I get some quiet time. Some people even carry a little microcassette with them and make verbal notes when they see things that interest them. I mean, it doesn't matter how you do it as long as you do it. There isn't a right and wrong way to get material—if you don't count copying stuff from

Comedienne Lily Tomlin.

a cable special and things like that. Or, you could have a baby. Kids are a great source of material and everyone can relate to it. Although I wouldn't recommend having a baby just to get a stand-up routine.

Q: What would mean "you've made it" to you.

A: Walking down the aisle in my Bob Mackie gown to collect my Oscar. Can I go now?

3

Education: College or No?

If you are just finishing high school or on the brink of a college career and would like to try stand-up comedy, you may ask, "Is college really necessary? Won't four years in college put me four years behind in being a stand-up comic?"

Is college necessary? In a word: *yes*! Anyway you can make it happen, always get more schooling. Show business has been around for a long time. It will be there when you finish college. Besides, continuing school need not eliminate your goal of being a stand-up comic. You can work on material in your local comedy club until you graduate and go comic full time. College has no counterpart as an environment in which to mature and grow. Most people who have earned a four-year degree consider their college days among the most treasured moments of their lives—even if they didn't put the degree to its intended use. Four years of college will not put you behind in the comedy biz. There are no time lines or report cards or age limits in this profession. No one cares when you started or how many hours you have invested in the craft. The only benchmark is: Are you funny? The more life experience you have, the more potential material you have to draw upon.

Another reason to go to college has little to do with degrees and courses of study: It has to do with life-style. A large part of being a working comic is being able to take the life-style. Traveling week after week, living in strange places with strange people is not easy. College helps to buffer the transition from living at home by allowing you to live on your own within certain campus restraints. Those years of living on campus will help prepare you for the road and make the life much easier than if you try to go directly from your parents' home into comedy.

Perhaps the most compelling reason to complete college is the most obvious: You may not always want to be a stand-up comedian. Many people have spent years trying to make it as a comic only to find that they really loved screen writing, or advertising, or being an agent, or teaching, or something totally unrelated to the performing arts. Having a degree automatically gives you a plan B if comedy doesn't turn out to be all you thought it would be. It is also much easier to go to school and graduate with your scheduled class than to try to earn a degree later in life.

Convinced that you want to go on to college; or at least complete college? Good! Now what courses can you take to help your comedy career? First of all, no college offers a degree program in stand-up comedy. There are, however, several related majors that will advance your career. The first, of course, is theater or drama. Courses of study for a theater major usually include acting, stage movement, improvisation, film acting, play reading, and creative writing. Some schools even offer a course pertaining to stand-up comedy. Such courses will help you become more comfortable and more confident with your own words on stage. Other useful majors are speech, communications, English, radio and television, and journalism. The important thing to do is look through the college catalogue and find out what courses are required to graduate with a particular major. Colleges and universities set up their courses of study independently; the courses one school expects of an English major may not be what another school expects. Look at the total curriculum with the idea that you will start and finish at this particular school. If you think you will not get enough background to help you become a comic; look for another school. But try to complete your college program where you started. Changing schools often mean a loss of credits, extra expense, and a delay in graduation.

It should be noted that stand-up comedy as an industry has attracted many professionals from nonperforming fields. It is not unusual to find a comedian who is also a lawyer, a teacher, an engineer, an artist, or a doctor (all types). Comedy tends to attract a certain personality rather than field of interest. People who have such professional degrees simply use their additional expertise in their act. They incorporate their observations on the law or medicine or the business world to make their act unique. It is also possible to have a little of both worlds: maintain a profession during the day and moonlight as a stand-up comic.

LIFE AFTER STAND-UP COMEDY

As was mentioned, should the time come when you want out of comedy, a degree represents the educational credentials to start another chapter of your life. You have the freedom to become a lawyer or teacher or doctor. You also have the option to stay in the field of stand-up comedy without actually being a comic.

Writing

What job is at the top of the charts to keep you in comedy without actually doing comedy? Writing! Some comics are great performers and so-so writers. Some comics are great writers and so-so performers. Some are good at both disciplines. The comedians who happen to be prolific writers can potentially create more material than they can use—and sometimes material that is good but would not work well with their stage personality. Such material can be sold to other comics. Many famous comedians buy material regularly, and some maintain a full-time writing staff. Why? Comedy superstars do a lot of appearances. They always need something new to say. The sheer volume of material necessary to keep them at the top of the heap requires more writing time than they could ever invest while keeping their public appearance schedules. So they buy jokes from other writers. Once a joke is sold, it is no longer the property of the author and may not be used in the author's act.

Writing other than joke material is also an option. As the comics move from place to place they can always be working on a book, a script, or an article of some sort. The medium is good discipline and a natural fit with their life-style, not to mention an excellent source of additional income if their work is published or put on option. Writers need not go to an office each day to create. Many writers use a pseudonym (pen name). This is especially helpful for the person writing something that might be compromised if associated with a comedian. With the purchase of a portable computer or word processor, your workplace can travel with you.

Writers who prefer to stay in one area will find any number of opportunities to use their skills in the traditional workforce. Writers create the scripts that corporations use for employee training films. Writers create brochure copy for businesses, write news releases, and

31

produce copy for radio and television advertising. Many corporations employ a staff of writers full time to produce informational material about their business. To get a feeling for the incredible scope of the writing field, consider that everything you read—from movie tickets to instruction sheets to brochures to novels—has to be written by someone. Words do not magically appear on the backs of cereal boxes or in pamphlets displayed on racks at the airport. They have to be conceived and written by a person.

Other fields for writers are advertising and public relations firms. A company that does not maintain an in-house advertising department sometimes hires an agency that specializes in creating business advertising. The agency either employs staff writers or utilizes free-lance writers as needed. For the writer who does not want to be tied to any one product or employer, free-lance work is the way to go. A free-lance writer is self-employed and works on a project basis. He or she is in the same boat as the comic, from a business perspective. Like the comic, the freelancer must constantly look for work and be flexible to different situations. It is a little riskier than having a full-time job, but it does allow variety. For example, the writer may successively create an industrial film script on safety, write an article on a real estate development for a trade magazine, and invent a short brochure for a children's theater. The freelance prices his or her own jobs, works at will, and maintains a home office. He or she generally has a deadline for completion of the work and guidelines for the content; other than that, he or she is autonomous. Free-lance writers must budget their time and money carefully. On most jobs, only a small deposit is paid when the work is contracted, with the balance due upon completion (and satisfaction of the buyer). A project may take several rewrites to achieve a finished product. The more time spent on corrections, the less time the writer has for soliciting new work. Like comedy, at first blush this seems like an easy, relaxed career. It's not. It is very high pressure and stressful until the writer builds a reputation for quality and has regular clients. In writing, as in comedy, work breeds work. The more people familiar with your skill, the more opportunities you will have to write.

Theater or Films

Another extension of stand-up comedy is professional acting or directing. This can mean anything from the stage to radio and TV to feature film. In fact, well-established comedians like to schedule their bookings so that they are available during casting season for the fall TV shows in Los Angeles. In turn, comedians who have already been cast in a TV show or film schedule their club bookings around their hiatus (or season break). Some comics keep a month or so free each year to do a play in a regional theater. This cross-over work, whether they are acting or not, helps them keep up skills they may not employ in stand-up and avoids comedy burnout.

It should be mentioned that not all working comics are in a financial position to take a month off the road to act in or direct a play. Live theater pay scales tend to be much lower per show than stand-up comedy rooms. Even if the comic just wants to hang around L.A. in the spring for the pilot casting, supporting oneself still must be addressed. It is difficult to get a part-time day job to cover expenses. Every waiter and his dog would like to get into the movies (or TV or anything) in Hollywood. Understandably, employers are reluctant to hire someone whom they know they will have to replace in a couple of months. There are comedy clubs in Los Angeles, but the number of comics wanting work compared to the number of slots available is on the order of

Steve Martin mimics singer Michael Jackson .

a grain of sand to a mountain. No comparison. However, those brave souls who want to take the risk try telemarketing (phone sales) and/or pizza delivery. These jobs may keep you in burgers for a couple of months and give you more flexibility in your schedule to go to auditions. For comics who have been working on the road for long periods, burnout can be a problem. The best way to get things perking again is to take a short break.

The Wrong Field?

Which brings us to another important consideration in the comedy business. Some comics jump headlong into stand-up and discover a key fact: They enjoy everything about comedy except performing. These artists find actual performance anticlimactic to writing, contract negotiation, marketing, booking, and career planning. The other side of this coin is that a number of comics are much better at selling their act than actually performing it. They lack the personality or charisma needed to connect with an audience. Their material may even be funny, but coming from them it sounds insulting or condescending. This is a particularly difficult position: First they must recognize the problem, which is not easy to do. Then they must be absolutely realistic about their career options and consider stepping down from the stage.

How do you know if you are starting to slide into the category of comic who should not be performing? For the comic who finds performing anticlimactic, the answer is easy—how do you feel after a show? If you enjoyed it and the audience was with you, you are doing OK. If performing just isn't any fun, think about not doing it. If that idea gives you a feeling of relief, then go ahead and hang up your microphone. Move on with no regrets.

For the comic who can't seem to connect with an audience, even with well-written material, the answers are not so clear-cut. Look for these clues that might mean the stage isn't for you:

- Several other comics on the bill get a great response from the crowd. You do your best material and extract only polite attention.
- Club owners who have booked you a couple of times seem to be avoiding your calls for work. If you do reach them by phone, they are hesitant about giving you any more work, or moving you up in the lineup, or increasing your pay.
- Wherever you go, you seem to have trouble getting along. The audience is too noisy or the club staff is too critical or the other comics bother you. Someone always seems to be in your face about something, making you angry a lot of the time.
- You realize you are frequently writing off an unresponsive audience as dumb or stupid.

If any of those sound familiar once you have ventured out on the road, have the courage to back off the stage. To continue in stand-up when it is a constant source of frustration will be painful. Besides, there are things you can do with your skills that don't involve performing. In addition to writing jobs, advertising agencies are always looking for bright new ideas. Radio, television, cable, and feature film production work might be an option. Becoming a booking agent for a comedy club is an alternative, or perhaps becoming an all-purpose talent agent or personal manager would suit you. Your background of performing, even if limited, will give you an eye for talent and an understanding of the needs of the performer. Last, but certainly not least, you could consider becoming a club owner. A comic who has spent even a little time on the road quickly gains an excellent overview of what is good and bad about club management. You would be in the unique position of being able to create a comedy room that would appeal to both the performers and the customers.

Remember, if you come to the realization that comedy is not for you, there's no shame in it. Few people end up at forty exactly where they thought they would be at eighteen or twenty. Life is a curvy road, not a precision stretch. Congratulate yourself for having the courage to be honest, and go forward.

4

The Good, the Bad, and the Funny of the Field

In Chapter 1 we looked at some of the positive and negatives of stand-up as they appeared at first glance. Now let's dig in and see what's beneath the surface. First the good news.

Stand-up comedy is a fun, highly visible craft. Comics are generally witty, interesting people with a zest for life that is intoxicating. Their work is always creative, never dull, and instantly gratifying. Comedians who do club work put in only an hour or so of actual stage time and maybe two or three hours of writing per day. Any way you slice it, they don't work eight-hour shifts. They don't have to wear a uniform or appear in business attire, and they can plan their lives around a schedule of their own design. Because of the travel involved, comedy is a wonderful adventure. One constantly meets new and interesting people (who, by the way, can be excellent sources of material). Technically, stand-up comedy is easy to do. You don't have to know how to operate a machine or program a computer or have a license. Except for the writing, no special skills are required. And, although we strongly encouraged college, when it comes down to the wire, you could do stand-up without the benefit of higher education. Not recommended, but possible. That's the good news.

THE DOWNSIDE

Now the bad news. As you read, there are literally hundreds (maybe thousands) of people trying to get started as comics. For every paid performing slot, there may be a dozen people to fill it. For every slot on a popular amateur night, there may be a dozen people waiting. This is a very competitive craft. For that reason alone, no one ever progresses as fast as they think they should.

Comedy material is all a comic has to "sell." Those thirty or forty minutes of jokes that comprise your act have been carefully and painstakingly cultivated. They belong to you alone. You make your living with them. Most professional comics follow an unwritten code that says a comic's act may not be used by another without permission from the author. I say *most* comics follow this code. There are, however, those who steal material. It's wrong. It's a dirty trick. It happens. And there is very little the comic can do about it. At best, he or she can try to reach the plagiarist and ask him/her to stop. At worst, he or she can start writing new material. Seeing or hearing of your material being snitched can be depressing.

Another notch on the bad side has to do with your emotional well-being. Stand-up comics have relatively no job security or benefits. If there is a legitimate reason for a club not to be open when you are contracted to appear there, you are out of luck and probably a paycheck. Perhaps the club had a fire or storm damage. The club owner would be sorry but could not possibly pay you when no show went on. Such legitimate, last-minute cancellations are written into many standard con-

39

tracts as "acts of God" or "hold harmless." (On the bright side, they can also work in the comic's favor should an unforeseeable problem arise.) The only health or dental insurance currently available to comics as a group is through the Professional Comedians Association. Members receive a discount on premiums.

Comedians lead a rather lonely life. They travel alone, work alone, and are their own best friend. It may not seem that way when you see them laughing and talking after a show, but it's true. Relationships are hard to maintain long distance, so they have brief encounters. A working comic is rarely in a position to invite friends over for dinner, go out on weekends, or join a special interest group. The comic's weekend is Sunday and Monday—sometimes just Monday. Comics see movies and ball games and have dates during the day. They meet acquaintances at restaurants and bars.

The constant travel necessary for the road comic can be very disorienting. If the pay is good, they spend some part of each week in an airport. If the pay is not so good, they spend part of each week driving to make the next engagement.

Even busy road comics have a home base, a place where their answering machine lives. However, *where* is another issue. Beginning comics can't live just anywhere (and still be able to make it financially). They have to live close to the work. That means living near a major metropolitan area that has several comedy rooms—which when you think about it isn't all that bad. Living in cities like Chicago, New York, Houston, or, of course, Los Angeles will help your career more than Bismarck, North Dakota. The beginning comic must be able to take off for an engagement on short notice. That means having a flexible day job that pays the bills when comedy bookings are lean.

As mentioned earlier, stand-up comedy and comedy

40

clubs as we know them are a new and old wrinkle at the same time. Because the industry is not yet standardized, there can be a great deal of inconsistency in how comics are treated, booked, housed, paid, and accepted by the community. Each geographical area tends to have its own idiosyncrasies. For example, New York comics may have a hard time playing to audiences in Mississippi, while Texas comics may not be well received in Colorado. Comics must learn to adjust or limit their work options. Along with the changes in geography come changes in how different people do the same thing: run a comedy club. For the beginning comic there are no "scale" payments or uniform minimums that can be paid to a performer as on a movie set or in a professional theater. There are no standard working conditions, overtime pay, or expense money beyond the talent and travel fees.

DEALING WITH REJECTION

Last, but not least, the comic needs to learn to deal with rejection. To the beginner (and even some veterans), it may seem that all the powers of the universe are throwing obstacles in your path. As soon as you think you have a solid twenty to thirty minutes, someone you respect will tell you that your act sucks. You try over and over again to reach a booker, do everything you are asked to do, and then are told they are not interested in your act. You showcase for a club owner, and are told to give it all up and go back to the ranch. You send out a videotape of your act, and a "Don't call us, we'll call you" letter comes back. Welcome to show business! In an industry with zillions more bodies than jobs, a lot of people are going to be rejected. Point of fact: Rejection will happen to you. What it does to you when it happens is entirely up to yourself and your attitude. You can become bitter and angry or see each rejection as a learning experience. As a beginning comedian you *must* believe in yourself because no one else is going to do it for you. The time you spend paying your dues (a cute phrase for being rejected) should decrease as time goes by. If you find that you are losing laughs or jobs or auditions, try to identify and correct what you can and don't worry about the rest.

Show business in general and comedy specifically can be such a paradox. One audience will love everything you say. Then, the same night, different show, different audience you can't get a smile. Who's to say why? The act was the same, the physical location the same, the people from the same community, and there you stood with both ends of the laugh meter in your lap for no apparent reason.

THE PRIVACY PROBLEM

Equally confusing is this: Comedians, even beginning comics, represent a kind of celebrity to an audience. After watching you, audiences often feel they know you personally. A part of your private life automatically goes when you become a public figure (even a minor one). The more successful you become, the less privacy you have. It is not unusual for a comic to be stopped on the street by a fan and asked to tell a joke for his friends; or to be expected to entertain the person sitting next to you on an airplane; or to have your meal at a restaurant interrupted so that someone can introduce you to his group. It is not an accepted practice for people to stop their accountant on the street and ask that he or she answer a tax question. A computer operator is probably never interrupted at dinner to run a few programs. Not so for the entertainer. Most show-biz folk learn to be gracious to overzealous fans; after all, they do mean well. Consider the intrusions a part of the package and go forward.

Another puzzle comes from the comics themselves. Most beginning comics will do anything to get jobs, go on the road, and be able to do comedy full time. The road is where the work is. The road is where you make contacts. The road is where you learn whether or not this is a career you want to pursue for the rest of your life. The road can make you or break you. But ask veteran comedians the one thing they wish they didn't have to do? Go on the road! Comics with several years of road work under their belts will do anything to find jobs close to home base.

Continuing, comedians who don't seem to have an introverted nerve in their body have unexplained attacks of shyness when asked to shake hands and mingle with an audience after a show. This seems to apply to beginners as well as veterans. The comic can demonstrate personality plus during all the booking phases, do excellent shows, seem to be a happy-go-lucky person, and then go into a full retreat after the show.

5

Useful Habits for the Stand-Up Comic

"Habit (hab'it), n. a thing done often and hence, done easily; practice; custom; act that is acquired and has become automatic." (*Websters New World Dictionary*)

Stand-up comedy, when it comes right down to it, is handmade and done alone. The habits you develop as even an amateur comic will stay with you for a long time. Since this is a voyage into uncharted waters for you, begin from day one to cultivate professional habits that will advance your career as you climb the ladder. You are going to cultivate something in any case; it might as well be positive rather than negative.

START A JOURNAL
First on your list: Create a system to capture ideas for new material as they occur to you. Start a journal—as large as a notebook or small enough to keep in your pocket or purse—to note things as they happen. Many comics carry a cassette recorder to make verbal notes. At the end of the day, take time to sit down with what you have gathered and write or record it in such a

fashion that you can remember the stimulus that sparked your attention in the first place. Some comics keep a card file, like a recipe box. Some keep audiotapes labeled by subject matter. Some comics write out the entire idea; some use their own form of shorthand. It doesn't matter how you do it; just that you do it.

Why do this at the end of each day? Your memory will be relatively fresh and you can recapture most of what struck you as funny. If you wait a few days to look over your notes, you may see an entry like "lizard lips" and wonder what you were thinking when you wrote it. At the end of a month or so, go back over your detailed notes. If the entry still seems funny, try to incorporate it into your act. If it turns out to have been funny at the time but not now, leave it alone. Don't throw it out. This little thought may help you with some other concept later on. Writing in your journal is something you should do throughout your career. No working comic, big or little, ever stops gathering material.

BUILD A CASH RESERVE

Second on your list, and more critical to the beginning comic than to anyone else: Start building a cash reserve. Open a separate savings account and force yourself to make regular deposits—even if it's only five bucks at a time. Realistically, to quit your job or school and go on the road, you need to save enough to live on if you had no money coming in for eight to ten months. Sit down with a calculator and add up *everything* you spend money on in a month: entertainment, newspapers, sporting events, office supplies, as well as food, rent, clothing, and car maintenance. Be realistic about your figures. When you believe you have a fairly detailed budget, make that amount the goal for your savings account. Once you make a deposit, forget about it and concentrate on making the next one. Don't consider that money available under any circumstances, and you won't be tempted to dip into it.

The reason for the savings account is that beginning comics cannot assume that they can live on comedy alone during the first year. The comic needs to be able to live—modestly, but live—and the savings account will give you some freedom to pursue your career. It is reasonable to assume that the beginning comic will not be booked into the highest-paying slots in the most prestigious rooms from the word go. Rather, he or she will start in smaller, limited-schedule (two or three nights a week), lower-paying rooms. Many limited-schedule rooms are in hotels, which means that comedy is not their only source of income. These rooms can come and go, sometimes for financial reasons, sometimes just because the hotel has changed managers. One manager may support the comedy concept, and the next one may not. If the incoming management does not, the comedy room folds. Closures, cancellations, and misunderstood bookings are fairly common at this level, but difficult for the comic to predict. The beginning comedian needs to be able to fall back on some kind of financial support should such a situation occur.

The nice thing about building this savings account is that the time it takes to grow will allow you to work out and hone your craft at the comedy clubs in your vicinity. At first, you will be taking bookings that are compatible with your work or school schedule, so building a savings account during this period should be a natural fit with your life-style.

RELATED COURSES
The next thing on your "To do" list, while you are still living at home base, writing in your journal, and adding to your savings account, is to take any performance- or writing-related courses or workshops that you can (a)

comfortably afford and (b) fit into your work/school/work-out schedule. Look for courses on acting, stage movement, speech/diction/public speaking, creative writing, and, most important, improvisation. Even if the course is designed to help stage actors with roles or business people with public speaking, or professional writers, take it. Apply as much as you can to stand-up, and leave the rest. These courses, especially improvisation, will help you be more comfortable inside your skin when you are on stage. They will broaden and enrich your knowledge of professional performing/writing.

Where do you find these courses? Colleges, of course, offer them as enrichment programs rather than degree prerequisites. Anyone in the community can take the courses, for a fee, and usually previous training is not required. Another source are professional and community theaters. Most have some kind of class almost always in progress. Teaching workshops or open classes can be a regular source of income for underpaid and overworked theater staff. The credentials of the teacher usually accompany any notice of the class. Also check the bulletin boards of any performing union or professional talent agent. These folks routinely post notices of workshops and classes offered by visiting professionals. Casting directors, film directors, and visiting authors sometimes offer one- or two-day seminars that can be very helpful to the fledgling comic.

You don't have to sign up for everything that comes down the pike. Take what you an afford without putting too much strain on your schedule. Short workshops or seminars are usually offered on weekends or in the evening, so you won't have to miss work or school to attend.

In the workshop department, watch out for organizations that promise to make you a star through their program. These groups will tell you that if you take all their classes, use their photographers, and pay them lots of money, they can help you become a big star. (The word "help" is usually in very small print in the contract.) Better to bypass these folks and save your money. You will do much better to nose around the performing community and see what is available through legitimate sources.

BUILD YOUR ACT

We mentioned earlier that keeping a journal of ideas was an invaluable habit for comedians. Along with your notes, you should force yourself to write one joke or segment of your act each day. Even if you don't think you'll ever use it, write it down. Why? The more material you flesh out from your journal, the further along you are toward developing an original, unique way of presenting your routine. Also, the physical act of writing at least one developed bit will keep you warmed up for performing. Like the professional singer who does scales every day, the writing of a completed concept keeps you in touch and feeling involved in the craft even on days when you can't perform. With this discipline, eventually you should start to see those funny little things you noticed and noted in your journal as developed jokes.

GATHER INFORMATION

The next habit on your list should be reading and information gathering. Read everything you can get your hands on. The written word is a tremendous source of material. Read a couple of newspapers a day and clip articles that might have some joke potential. Follow political campaigns and trends in music and food and sports. Know what is going on in the entertainment world. Watch TV news, and keep up on fashions. Read a best seller (fiction or nonfiction) a month. Stay abreast of the latest pop psychology movement, scientific discoveries, and medical break-throughs. Go to the movies and read magazines that don't play "to type." That means if you are a guy who reads *Field & Stream* or *GQ* start reading *Cosmopolitan*. If you are a woman who reads *Vogue* and *Golf Magazine*, pick up a copy of *Veterans*. See what gets written on the other side of the coin. Even if you don't agree politically with a publication, it should generate new thoughts and potential new material.

PEOPLE-WATCHING

When you are not reading, watch. Watch people doing regular, everyday people stuff. Sit in a mall and study the people you see there. Pretty soon you will be amazed at the wonderful idiosyncrasies we humans develop. You will start to see things that you have totally missed in first-glance observation. The people who are too vain to wear their glasses and try to squint their way through the shopping center. The different ways moms bribe their kids to cooperate. The point at which husbands start to whine when they have been brought shopping only to be the pack animal. What kinds of people shop at which stores. The difference between day shoppers and night shoppers. In short, people-watch whenever you get the opportunity. Do it in the grocery store, at sporting events, in parks, in nightclubs—wherever you happen to be.

GOAL-SETTING

One last habit that you need to begin is the process of goal-setting. Remember, comedy careers are like little industries. Like a manufacturer, you need to have a business plan that includes realistic stepping-stones for yourself. Obviously, to say, "I want to start comedy this month and be making $5,000 a month next month," is not practical. Start by telling yourself how many new lines you would like to write each week. When you reach that goal fairly regularly, add something else. Make each new goal a little harder than the last. Consider everything in the comedy business a learning experience until you can predict the outcome regularly. On the average, it takes a beginning comedian about a year to get the first twenty to thirty minutes of solid, proven comedy material. The operative word here is "average." Some beginners move very quickly into the comedy workforce, and some more slowly. The important thing is not to beat yourself up and become bitter if someone who started at about the same time you did seems to be moving faster. That attitude is counterproductive. If you miss a few benchmarks, back up and try again.

A helpful step toward reaching your goals is to have a firm grasp of what constitutes your on- and off-stage persona. Many performers never know when to turn off the stage personality and turn on the real person. They stay at a frenzied pitch for days and then crash and burn at the first turbulence. These folks are easy to recognize. They are always "on," always telling a bit rather than having a conversation, always hustling. If confronted, they say that they are ambitious and aggressive. They say that one has to be that way to succeed in show business. True, you need ambition and assertiveness in this business. You need to maintain steady forward movement to go the distance in show business. The people with the tremendous highs and lows wear themselves out before they really start to do something with their comedy.

6

Taking the First Steps

If you have carefully evaluated the pros and cons of stand-up comedy that have been discussed so far *and* you think you have the personality and temperament for it and you still want to be a comic, you're ready for the next step: watching. But wait, you say. All I've done so far is write and evaluate and look at people and save money. When do I get to do the comedy? When do I get to try my wings on stage?

It's all well and good to intellectualize about this craft and the life-style. It is another thing entirely to go to a comedy club, absorb the ambiance, see real comics at work, and imagine yourself in their shoes. Before you even mention to the comedy club manager that you might be interested in amateur night, before you say a word on stage, do the following:

GO WATCH
Visit the full-time comedy rooms, the one-night rooms, amateur nights, and comedy contests. Go to every local comedy function you can find. Travel as far as you can, within reason, and watch comedy clubs and amateur nights in other cities. Don't watch to get material;

watch to see *how they do it*. Why are some successful with the crowd and some not? How does their energy level affect how the material is received? What do they wear? What kind of material gets the best response? Which ones can you imagine seeing on a talk show some day? Which ones seem to write better than they deliver? Do they seem to enjoy what they are doing? Which seem tired? (This is important to recognize because you may have to see it in yourself some day.) Did you hear something you've never heard before, or was everything slightly familiar? What is consistent about all of them? What isn't?

If you live in a city that has several comedy clubs and is home base for a number of comedians, try following a comic from room to room. See how the comedian adjusts the same material in different rooms. When comics are getting laughs, it's easy to be on stage, but what happens when a show bombs? How do the comics handle a bad show? Absorb as much as you can of what you see. Make journal entries of what you see. Sit all over the room and see how position affects your perception of how the comic is doing. What do you notice sitting in the back of the room that you didn't sitting in the front row? ("I could see better in the front" doesn't count.) Come up with your own questions that you want answered at each performance you see.

There are reasons for all this watching: To be a professional comic you have to work at it every chance you get, which means a time investment. If you only feel like going out to watch once a week or so, you don't have it. If you can't get out to watch because of family, job, or school commitments, stay where you are and tend to your responsibilities. It is realistic to assume that if you can't make time to go watch every night, you can't invest the time it takes to get started in the business.

Another reason for watching: To be a professional comic you have to be passionate about the craft and be able to handle the life-style. If you are bothered by smoke-filled rooms that serve alcohol, forget about being a stand-up comic. If you are basically a day person and wouldn't want to change that part of your routine, stand-up comedy is not for you. If just watching the life-style offends you, think what living it would be.

Still another reason for watching: Going from room to room, even to see the same acts, will give you an idea of the adjustments comics make on every stage, before every audience. No two shows are ever the same. You may hit a consistent stride, but you will not give identical performances. Sometimes the adjustments the comic needs to make are slight, sometimes basic. Develop an eye for these things, and make observations as to why the comic had to make the adjustment. If you are not sure, go up to the comic after the show and ask. You will be surprised at the simplicity of the answer compared to the impact it had on the show. Maybe the comic just pumped up the delivery a little to excite a late-night crowd. Maybe the comic first improvised with the audience to see what kind of subject matter appealed to this group. Maybe the comic did everything "bigger" to accommodate a big room; or "smaller" for a more intimate room.

In some states the liquor laws require that comedy club audiences be of legal drinking age. If this is the case, you may have to pursue other avenues to watch. First, of course, are TV, cable, feature films, and radio programs. A great deal of comedy programming uses stand-up comics. Watch these, and note when you see the same comic on several different programs. Did the comic change his or her set? What was different or the same about this program compared to the others?

In some metropolitan areas non-nightclub establishments sometimes sponsor talent contests that include stand-up comics. Go watch these. See if you find any familiar faces competing. Rent classic movies or TV shows featuring late, great comics. Video houses and libraries have good selections of classic comedy: Charlie Chaplin, the Marx Brothers, Lucille Ball, Peter Sellers, Burns and Allen, Jack Benny, Jonathan Winters. While these artists are (and were) not all stand-up comedians, they are all masters of comedy. Watch the old videos with the same questions you had of the live performers. Watch the technique and timing. Always watch the video twice—once to get the story out of the way and once to watch the performance.

Another avenue for research is contemporary comics who have made an album, a concert video, or a cable special. The roster of celebrity comedians grows each day, but work by Robin Williams, George Carlin, Lenny Bruce, Sam Kinison, Emo Phillips, Richard Pryor, Eddie Murphy, and many more is all readily available to the comedy buff. Note that the material is different, the personality is different, but all have a unique inner voice that sets them apart from their contemporaries.

FIND A STAGE

Now that you have watched comics and still want to pursue this craft, start working on finding a place to perform. Most young comics start on amateur nights at a local comedy club. Comedy clubs with an amateur night have specific guidelines for open-mic talent to follow. Call the club to find out what rules apply for amateurs. Most clubs have a specific sign-up policy, which usually involves calling in advance to sign up for a limited number of performance slots available. Generally, amateur comics are given five minutes of stage time each time they get on stage, or "go up."

Time your material at home at about the delivery speed you intend to use so that you hit your limit or less. Young comics who consistently go over time on stage find it more and more difficult to get subsequent slots. Many clubs have a "drop list" of people who are no longer allowed to sign up for slots. There are several ways to get on such a list, and consistently going over time is one of them. Most clubs also have basic rules of conduct for amateurs who go up. These are generally common-sense, good-manners rules like "Don't destroy the stage" or "No hitting the customers." Find out the rules and follow them. Most managers would rather have you ask up front what the limits are than to have to bounce you from the club for misconduct.

If you live in a city that has open stage nights in a number of places, work all of them. Get on stage as often in as many rooms as possible each week. Each room will have a different feel and a different clientele. Start learning to adjust. If you are immediately comfortable on a stage, you can concentrate on making your material work. Audiences can smell fear. If a strange sound system or a broken piece of equipment can upset you, the audience will be less likely to laugh. They get nervous for you. If you can relax, they can too, and your laugh quotient will go up a few points.

If you live in a city that has no comedy club or entertainment room to work out of, you have three options: (a) move, (b) postpone your career until you are in a position to move, or (c) see if you can start an amateur stand-up comedy night in an existing club (assuming the owner will allow possibly underage people to enter) or a student facility currently using live talent. Developing your own comedy night will be a great deal of work, but it will satisfy your immediate need for a performance place, especially if you are too young to get into a working club. However you do it, the beginning comic must have stage time. There is no substitute for being on stage in front of an audience several times a week.

If you are going to approach a working nightclub for stage space, suggest starting an amateur night on a slow or off night for the venue. If this is not possible, suggest that the amateurs be allowed to go up during band breaks or, in a sports bar, after the game. Tell the owner that amateurs traditionally bring their friends to see them perform, which can mean more customers. They are also good at word-of-mouth advertising, and since they are not paid, there is no overhead.

If you approach a school facility for a performing space, be sure that school officials recognize the need for an amateur comedy night on campus. Be willing to assume the responsibility for getting the project off the ground and to invest the time and energy to keep it flying. If you are given permission to use a campus facility, organize your friends to help manage and promote the event. Enlist support from student publications, social organizations (fraternities/sororities/professional associations), and appropriate school departments (theater, English, journalism). Pass out flyers, get on the campus radio, and encourage special-interest groups to attend in a body. Last, but certainly not least, use the facility and equipment with care. Nothing will curtail such a project faster than holes punched in the walls, broken equipment, and dirty premises. This sounds like a tremendous undertaking, and it is. But for the amateur in search of a comedy stage where none currently exists, it is crucial.

Once again, there is no substitute for stage time for the young comic. What was said about moving or planning to move was not facetious. It is a reality to the fledgling comedian. If you can't move or create a comedy stage, you can't have a career in this field.

MAKE THE BEST OF AMATEUR STATUS

Once you have found a stage and secured a slot as an amateur in the lineup, there are three things you should do every time you go up from now until they ask you to be Jay Leno's permanent replacement: (a) tape record every show; (b) ask someone you trust to watch you and give you feedback; and (c) write. After they've offered you Jay's job, you can drop (a) and (b).

Why tape record? Performing a stand-up brings a terrific rush of adrenalin. Most comics, even the ones who couldn't have gotten a laugh with a machine, leave the stage thinking they "killed" or at least did a great job. A tape recording heard the next day may give an entirely different perspective.

Could you understand every thing you said? If you are not sure, see if someone who doesn't know your act understands every word. Did one laugh cover the setup for another so that you lost the second laugh? Was the setup so long that by the time you got to the punchline it fell flat? Are you talking too fast? Too slow? If you have a noticeable accent, is it getting in the way? Where is the audience laughing? Are they laughing where you thought they should? *Are they laughing?* Are they groaning? Tape recordings don't lie. If you did as well as you thought, the tape will back you up. If not, take a deep breath, listen to what really happened, and make the necessary adjustments. Tapes are the kindest way to learn from a bad set. You may have to hone your craft in front of the public, but there is no reason why you can't improve your odds by rehearsing in private like other performing artists. You have to grow or go in this business!

Why have someone watch you? Same as above, plus the following: A person may be able to tell you *why* some of the material didn't work. A person may help you see that a particular part of your routine is too dirty, too vague, too long, too post peak, too short, underexplained, etc. A person may also be able to suggest some shift in placement of material that would strengthen your act. When choosing a person, look for someone who has had more success at stand-up than you have and whose material you respect. If other comics are not available, try to get the club manager or owner to catch your act every now and then.

As a word of caution, don't be discouraged if the club owner or manager won't watch your act every time you ask. Running the comedy club at night is their workday. Also, don't get down on yourself if you receive conflicting advice from two of your experts. Taste in comedy is personal. Take all the feedback graciously and integrate what makes the most sense to you. Over a period of time, the audience will tell you what works and what doesn't. In any event, understand that if you have asked someone for an opinion of your act, you must be prepared to take whatever response you get. Becoming defensive or angry defeats the purpose of asking for feedback.

Why write all the time? Writing is the most important tool of your craft. The more you write, the better writer you become. If you live to be a thousand and have been reincarnated as Jay's replacement, you will never have enough material.

Find Material

"But where do I start?" you ask. "How do I put together even five minutes of stand-up material to test?" I am not going to explain how to write stand-up comedy material—few people can. The spirit of the comic, that innate sense of humor, cannot be taught. It's a gift, like perfect pitch or a sense of rhythm. Many workshops and coaches claim to teach stand-up comedy. Not true. Stand-up comedy cannot be taught. Performing techniques can be taught—how to hold a microphone, how to move on stage. In fact, as was mentioned earlier, most bookers encourage young comics to take acting or stage movement or, better yet, a basic improvisation class to gain technical skills. Composition skills can be taught—how to construct a sentence, how to edit. But the comedy part, the part that makes even simple gestures funny, comes from within. The comic, quite simply, thinks in terms of funny. You either have it or you don't. If you have it, you can enhance and develop it with time in front of an audience. If you don't, go back to what you do best as soon as you can.

Good material, however, seems to have two ingredients: originality and uniqueness. The subject matter can be anything you like as long as your perspective on it is completely original. Original in this context means two things: (1) Everything you say must belong to you (you either wrote it or purchased it). "Borrowing" material from another writer or comic, even to get started, is totally unacceptable. (2) The material you perform is as unique as you are. Your material should reflect your individual voice. Generic comics—comics who are sort of funny but you can't remember much else about them—are just that, generic. If you want to stand out, your material must stand out.

The first place to look for subject matter is your journal, which was discussed in Chapter 5. Take out the journal and read through the entries. Choose five or six items that interest you and work on developing them for your act.

Another avenue for material is good, old-fashioned people-watching. Hang out at the mall, sit in a park, be observant at a concert, family reunion, or office party. Left to their own devices, people do very interesting things. While you are watching people, listen at the same time. Regional accents and life-styles are different:

An example is the Northerner who "gets ready" for something as opposed to the Southerner who is "fixin' to go." We are a diverse populace with cross-cultural backgrounds. That means there is potential material around every corner if you are observant enough to spot it.

When you have pinned down the subject matter you want to work on, there are a few mechanical tips in the writing:

In comedy, less is always more. Young comics tend to overwrite or overexplain a joke. They think that if a laugh was not forthcoming, the audience didn't understand what was said. So they add more and more words until the premise grows but the laugh quotient is diminished. The fewer words the better. Here's an example, using a very old joke: "Guy walks into a diner and asks the cook, 'Do you serve hamburgers here?'. Cook says, 'Sure, we serve anybody.'" Less is more. That isn't the funniest joke ever written, but it's a joke. Imagine how *unfunny* it would be this way: "A man walks into a little neighborhood restaurant. He sees the cook standing behind the counter, gets his attention, and asks if hamburgers are served at this diner. The cook thinks about it, then says, 'Of course, we do. We have a complete menu for all kinds of people.'" Less is more.

Comics may often use the same topics, but the material needs to be from a personal perspective. You may have heard comics talk about relationships, parents, school, driving, music, and so on. The difficult task is to find something unique about your experiences with those topics.

Write with your stage persona in mind. How are you going to deliver this joke? High-energy and fast-paced like Robin Williams, or slow and deadpan like Steven Wright? Will you be doing your act as character or as your real self? Would the joke be enhanced by an audiovisual aid (prop), or musical instrument, or magic, or mime, or juggling?

The best way to encourage a club owner to give you subsequent stage slots, after your first one, is to make the audience remember you. The best (and cheapest) way to promote yourself is to be sure the audience leaves remembering your name.

HAVE PATIENCE, PERSISTENCE, FAITH IN YOURSELF

This can be an extremely frustrating business. Just when you think you are really funny, a pro comes along and tells you you're a hack. You may not always get a performance slot when you want one. You may have a long string of sets with what seems little improvement. You may have writer's block that keeps you from developing new material. In fact, many professional comedians say that during those first few months they seemed to "run out of things to say." Every idea was securely in the grasp of another comedian. Comics who started after you may be progressing faster.

Keeping a realistic artistic goal in front of you is extremely important at this point in your career. This is guaranteed to be a difficult period for you as a comic. More than likely you are working or going to school all day, in a comedy room each night, and running into yourself in between. Take things at a pace that you can manage. There are no report cards or deadlines in this business other than the ones you impose upon yourself. An audience is *never* concerned with how long it took you to be funny. You're ready when you're ready—kind of like learning to walk. On the average, it takes six months to a year for a comic to work up the first twenty to thirty minutes of solid comedy material. If you give up and quit, no one will take you by the hand and beg you to become an amateur comic again.

61

The persona Whoopi Goldberg created for herself, at the Lyceum Theatre, in 1984.

Take extra care to eat well and exercise during this period. Be patient (comedy stars aren't made overnight), be persistent (discipline yourself to keep working), and have faith in yourself (right now you may be the only one who thinks you're funny—but one is better than no one).

If you've read this far and are not scared off by the enormous time commitment plus the potential for repeated rejection and humiliation, hat's off to you! Read on—the journey is just beginning.

7

Tools of the Trade

So you think you are ready to hit the road. You were an amateur for a while and then moved up to regular in your developmental room: Your act has improved, the club owner or manager has given you more stage time, and you can go up on nights other than amateur nights. Let's say you have about twenty minutes of good material, and you want to try for a booking at a club for money. What's the next step?

Any person who wants to be booked as a professional stand-up comedian should have the following promotional materials available to the booker or club owner: a current photograph, a brief résumé of your performing career, and several audition tools.

THE PHOTOGRAPH

Your promotional photograph should be an 8 × 10, black-and-white "headshot." This means one showing you, as you look today, from about the neck up. Comedians who perform in costume, with musicians or other back-up, might want to take a full-length shot, but that is generally not necessary.

Have the photograph taken against a light background. Some clubs use headshots as art in their advertisements. Newspaper reproduction tends to make pictures look muddy. The light background will make your face stand out. This rule applies to all races, the only exception being a person with a very light complexion and blonde hair. In such case the background can lean toward a gray-flannel hue, but never all the way to black.

All your photographs should have your name printed at the bottom. This is an absolute must! Booking agents and club owners are bombarded by comedians. They will not remember your name or face from an audition. A picture without a name signals to the booker that this is an amateur or a person with very little experience.

To get the right photograph, you must first find the right photographer: (a) someone you can afford, and (b) someone who is good at black-and-white "people" shots. You can find such a photographer by asking more experienced comics. Or you could ask a talent agent for a recommendation. (Talent agents are the people who represent actors/actresses/models for TV commercials, movies, and so on. They almost always know of good, inexpensive photographers for headshots.) When you have several names, go to see the photographers' sample books. Don't make a commitment to anyone until you have seen several books. As you look at the samples, you should be looking for good, clean (not shadowy) black-and-white shots of *people*. See if the photographer has captured something that tells you something about the subject. Does he or she look happy, upbeat, tired, ill—anything defined will do. If you get no sense of definition from the picture, perhaps you should keep looking. Some photographers are very good with color but just don't have an eye for black-and-white. If the photographer has no black-and-white samples in the book, definitely keep looking. It also helps if you like

65

and feel comfortable with the photographer. This person will have to translate your ideas about your head-shot into tangible form. Communicating well with the photographer is very helpful.

In selecting your photographer, find out in advance what the fee is and what is included in a "session." A session is the hour or so you will spend with the photographer actually taking the pictures. During this session the photographer will generally shoot a roll of film (36 pictures), allow you to change clothes at least once, and allow you to choose from one to three prints for one price. The photographer may also try to sell you makeup and hair design for the picture. Use your own judgment on adding these extras with this in mind: The end result should be a natural, *as you look now*, picture. If you are going for a "regular person" look on stage, that is the type of shot you should take. Glamour shots are more appropriate for models. A short time after the session, the photographer will give you a contact sheet, a developed piece of photographic paper showing the entire roll of film in miniature. You will need a mag-nifying glass to see detail on this sheet. From the contact sheet, select the number of pictures included in your session fee to be blown up into prints. You may select more prints than are included in your fee for an additional charge. Find out the cost of extra prints before you order them; you may want to wait a while before ordering extra prints for financial reasons. The photographer will develop one copy of each print you order. Normally you will not receive the negatives; keeping the negatives and charging for additional copies is a legitimate source of income for the photographer.

After you have selected the print(s) you like, find a company that mass-produces photographs. Why? You will need about 75 to 100 pictures to start. If you purchase these prints from the photographer at several

Steven Juliano Moore

Steven Julian Moore is a working stand-up comedian living in Texas. (His personal address and phone number have been deleted from this photograph.)

dollars each, the tab will much be higher than if you use a mass production company working at cents on the dollar per print. These companies are listed in the phone book under Photo Finishing. The mass production company can cheaply reproduce any number of copies from an existing print. The more you order, the cheaper. Be prepared to pay for one negative per print (this one you can keep); typesetting your name at the bottom of the picture; and prints. Your completed order will include an envelope containing your negative and a "guide print" from which additional prints can be made. Keep these flat in a cool, dark place.

With your pictures in hand, use them as business people use their business cards. Keep a supply handy and pass them out freely. Above all, don't treat them as a precious commodity that only a few people can have.

The pictures should be in your possession before you make a first call to a booking agent. The comedian, or would-be comedian, who says, "Look, I'm having some pictures made—book me and I'll send them to you," is telling the booker three things. First, the pictures haven't been shot and may never be shot; the comic wants to use the first few jobs to finance the photography session. Second, there is a strong possibility that this comic will never send promotion in time to be used by the club. Third, who needs this comic! Borrow the money if you have to, but have your promotional materials in place from day one. Some bookers cancel an act that does not send promotional materials within the designated time, and they are well within their rights. People who wish to be treated and paid as professionals should behave professionally.

THE RÉSUMÉ OR BIO

The résumé or biography (bio) is a one-page overview of you and your experience in the comedy business. It should *always* have your name, address, and current phone number. If a booker can't reach you by phone or mail, you have wasted your efforts to get a booking.

"But I've just started my career!" you say. "I don't have any professional credits." If your performing career consists only of a string of amateur nights, you still need a bio, a short, interesting paragraph or two about yourself that the club owner can use to promote you. (The key word is interesting.) Where did you grow up? Do you have any special skills? What do you do for fun, that's printable? Interests, hobbies, degrees? All club owners and bookers know that everyone has to start somewhere. If you are requesting opening positions, they will not expect you to have tons of performing credits.

If you are writing a biography, try to be funny. Remember, this is a comedian's bio—it should be clever and reflect your personality. This biography or résumé, your picture, and your audition are the basis for a potential employer's first impression. Make it a good one.

A résumé may also include interesting tidbits about your life, but it should contain a list of the comedy clubs you have played. In writing a résumé, be truthful. This is a very clannish business. If you say that you have headlined a room when you haven't (and obviously don't have the capability), you could burn a bridge for a very long time.

After you have written your résumé or bio, have it typed on a good typewriter, word processor, or computer with a good quality printer. Check the document for grammar, spelling, and style. Always have a friend proofread it. When you are satisfied with what you have written, photocopy it on *light* paper—for the same reason you used a light background for your pictures. Booking agents keep a file of talent used regularly. They

69

Maurine Harker:
The Story No One Wants to Hear

When Maurine Harker decided to become a stand-up comedian she already had a career. (Two careers, if you count feeding, driving, clothing, driving, housing, driving, washing, driving, buying for, and did I mention, driving around two children) With an MA in Journalism from Northwestern University, Maurine had been teaching for the Harris Jr. College system for ten years when it occurred to her. If she was going to be entertaining a group of people each day, why not get paid slightly bigger bucks for the effort. Why not try comedy!

And she did. She has played comedy clubs and bars and picnics and breakfast meetings and schools and, believe it or not, a slumber party. She has been laughed at by young people, old people, church people, Republicans (if that's possible), and this guy in Tama who thought she was so funny that he wanted to give her his glass eye. Last year Maurine won the Funniest Person in Harris contest. She used her prize money to buy a new battery . . . she won't say what size or for what.

Maurine's material is clean, high-energy, with the sort of observations about life that make people say, "When that happened to me, I shot the guy." Maurine's sense of humor is perfect for women's groups, men's groups, and combinations of the two. If you'd like to watch Maurine do her stuff, come to The Funny House in Harris where she is house MC every other week through 1993.

Maurine Harker, teacher, mother, collector of pecan pie recipes, swimmer, zoo volunteer, expert marksman, and darn good spot washer, is about as funny as they get. Come watch her show before the tickets get too expensive.

Maurine Harker
124 Main St. Harris,
TX 00000
Service: (713) 000-0000

STEVEN JULIANO MOORE
2630 Fountainview Suite 300
Houston, TX 77057
(000) 000-0000

About Comedian Steven Juliano Moore: Steven has been a favorite on the college circuit for over ten years. The NEW YORK TIMES described him as "an accomplished comedian." His comedy has been quoted in NEWSWEEK and FORUM, and his routines featured in the Book of the Month Club selected novel *COLD KILL* by Jack Olson. As a headliner in nightclubs, Steven has appeared, literally, all over the United States, Canada, and the Caribbean. His unique sense of humor, up-to-the-minute material, and high-energy delivery leave audiences roaring and make Steven an often requested performer.

CLUBS
(Representative List)

FUNNY BONE	Knoxville, TN & Lafayette, LA
THE COMEDY WORKSHOP	Houston & Austin, TX
SIR LAUGHS ALOT	Nashville, TN
JOKERS	Oklahoma City, OK
COMEDY IN AMERICA	Washington D.C.
CRACKERS	Indianapolis, IN
CONCORDIA UNIVERSITY	Montreal, Canada
WEST PALM BEACH COMEDY CLUB	West Palm, FL
PUNCHLINE	Columbia, SC & Montgomery, AL
VIRGINIA BEACH COMEDY CLUB	Virginia Beach, VA
BIRMINGHAM COMEDY CLUB	Birmingham, AL
JOLLY'S	Amarillo, TX
THE COMEDY ATTIC	Rochester, NY
THE FUNNY FARM	Buffalo, NY
SEVEN SAILS COMEDY CLUB	Grand Cayman, BWI
CHARLEY GOODNIGHTS	Raleigh, NC
COCONUT'S AMERICAN COMEDY CLUB	London, England

and
ARTS AND ENTERTAINMENT NETWORK:
COMEDY ON THE ROAD, 1992

More about Moore: Steven Juliano Moore has toured with Lola Falana, Tom Rush, B.B. King, Jose Feliciano, Graham Nash, Gordon Lightfoot, and many others. In addition to playing nightclubs, Steven is known for his convention work, writing special material for some of the country's major corporations. During his many years as Comix Annex Artistic Director for Houston's famed Comedy Workshop, Steven conducted stand-up comedy workshops and lectured on comedy writing at the University of Houston.

Résumé of an experienced comedian.

will expect you to keep supplying them with pictures, but they can always make photocopies of your resumé and/or bio. If you send an original on dark-colored paper, the copy will be close to unreadable. If you must use colored paper for your printed materials, use pastels or off-white.

As you progress in your career, other kinds of promotional items can be employed for self-promotion: tri-fold brochures, large foil-stamped folders to hold promotional packets, postcards, buttons, and posters. It is also a good idea to keep booking agents and club owners up-to-date on your credits with current booking upgrades, reviews, and articles. Most of these items will need to be laid out by a professional printer, typesetter, or embosser. Prices will vary according to the grade of paper you select, number of photographs used, amount of color, number of copies, amount of cutting and folding, size, amount of typesetting, and postage. Get a complete price quotation from design to delivery, so that you know exactly what you are getting into. Bells and whistles are nice, but you can have a very good career with clean, clear updated headshots, resume/bio, and current reviews and/or articles. Bookers and club owners hire funny people, not expensive printing.

AUDITION TOOLS

A comedian is hired for a first job in one of several ways: (1) Live audition or showcase; (2) strong recommendation from a trusted source; (3) piggyback booking with another comic; or (4) videotape audition.

The live audition is self-explanatory. Arrange with the club owner or booker to perform a short set at a place of their choosing. After your set, you will either be told to call at an appointed time for bookings, or that they are going to pass on your act. If a booking is not offered, it is fine to ask for pointers from the person

SHARON GERRIE

GO AHEAD! SHOOT HER...

MAKE HER YOUR DAY PLAYER.

SHARON GERRIE

ACTRESS
CHARACTER
CHARACTER VOICE
MODEL

ACTORS ETC.
(713) 785-4495

Postcard used as a marketing tool.

who has showcased you. It will do you little good to get angry or whine. Better to take the decision gracefully and ask how long you should wait before approaching the booker again. Whatever happens, *do not* leave the stage saying, "That wasn't as good as I usually do." *Do not* list a number of things that "threw you." Don't make apologies. They weaken you in the eyes of the decision-maker and lessen your chances of a repeat audition. Bookers want a comic who can consistently do the job under a variety of circumstances. If you can work in only one environment, you're not ready for a first job.

Occasionally a club owner or booker will book you on the basis of a strong recommendation from a colleague, usually another owner or booker, or a comedian the club owner books frequently and trusts. A piggyback booking assumes that these people trust each other's judgment, which is a big assumption in this business. It means that a booker is taking the recommendation of another that you are funny. If the recommendation comes from another comedian, it assumes that (a) you are funny and (b) the two of you together will produce a good show. Recommendation bookings are risky for everyone. If you do poorly, not only will you probably not get future bookings, but the person who recommended you could be hurt professionally as well.

Finally we come to the videotape audition. This is probably the most common form of audition available to the comic, the booking agent, and the club owner. The videotape audition allows the comic to submit a set that is representative of the quality of his or her work. It also allows the booking agent or club owner to audition privately, at a convenient time.

The video audition is a fifteen- to twenty-five-minute tape of your act. This length of time is sufficient for the beginning comic or one who is approaching a booker for the first time and requesting an opening or feature position. Headline comedians are usually asked to submit a longer set—forty-five to fifty-five minutes. The video should be on ½-inch VHS, and the tape should be rewound and "clean." That means that when the viewer plugs the tape into the machine, the first thing seen should be either an identification card for you or you yourself beginning your set. The tape should *not* begin with a three-minute leader from an old movie because you used one from your files and didn't bother to proof it. Such a tape is one less for the booker to watch.

To make an audition tape, you need to find someone with a home video recorder that can tape several sets on several nights, or hire a professional. Professional camera people will do a good job, but an audition tape for club work does not need broadcast quality. A clear home recording, shot from one angle, with nonstatic sound will do the job. Put together the cleanest, clearest tape you can for the lowest possible price. Remember, you will need to upgrade the tape every six to eight months or as your act changes significantly. Don't put all your money into the first one and have nothing left for six months later.

When you have several recordings of your set, watch all of them and select the one you like the best. Perhaps ask a trusted comic friend or significant other to view them and give you feedback. Make sure that you can be seen and that *everything you say can be heard*. If you have to choose between a tape in which you look slick and a tape with clear sound—go for the sound. Bookers do not expect broadcast quality tapes, but they do need to hear everything you say. The tape you end up with is your original, or master tape. You are now ready to have copies or "dubs" made from your master tape.

In the phone book under Audio/Video Production

Services, look for a company that does audio/video reproductions. Call several companies and ask how much they charge for about two dozen dubs from a master (including the actual tape). Production houses can dub tapes the same way photocopiers make copies: fast and cheap. When you have found a company you like, take the master to them and have the duplications made all at one time. When you get the tapes back, be sure to store the master tape like your master headshot: in a cool dry place out of harm's way. Never send out your master tape. Take the time and make a duplicate. Ask the price if you supply the tape; some companies reduce the price if you supply tape, but only use certain brands on their machines. Most services offer additional services like sky blue leader on the tape before your set, computer graphic identification before and/or after your set, and labels. Be sure to check the prices of these items before you agree to them. Production houses price per dub, the same way photocopier houses price per sheet of paper. A dub that is $6 plus $1 for each I.D. sounds cheap for one and expensive at $168 for twenty-four.

If you are on a strict budget, you may dub off your own videotape copies. Rent or borrow a second VCR and record a second copy from your master. Buy and print your own labels, or use the labels that come with the blank tape. However you produce your videotape audition, two things are essential: *Always* put your name, address, and phone number both on the tape and on the cover. As with your photograph, you must identify yourself on the outside of the tape for the booker to put a face to an act. Bookers sometimes watch twenty tapes at a sitting. Make your name and act easy to remember.

Never, never, never put time and money into an edited tape. An edited tape is one with pieces of several sets, shot at different times. An edited tape that cuts from set to set is a signal to a booker that some parts of your act are so bad that you couldn't get a good response from several audiences. When a booker asks to see a tape of your act, it means a tape of the act *intact*.

The last consideration of the videotape audition is the attitude a comic should have about a request for a tape. It is not an insult when a booker asks you for a tape. This is standard operating procedure for most bookers. It is much more convenient for the booker to showcase from videotape than live performance, and a booker can see as many comics and give more time to each on tape as from live showcase. A booker looks at a tape for more than one reason. You may have a list of references good enough for canonization, but the booker needs to see your act. The booker will want to see your style, listen for energy level, and get a feel for your material. A good booker puts shows together with variety in mind. You may be a very funny, low-energy comic, but on a bill with another very funny, low-energy comic the show will drag and the club will suffer.

When the request for a tape is made, ask the booker how much time he or she takes to view tapes. Don't call back in two weeks if the booker said two months. Make a note in your datebook to follow up at the time indicated. Some bookers send form letters back to comics stating what they can or cannot do for them. If the booker indicates that a letter will be sent after the tape has been viewed, don't plague him or her with phone calls. If you are asked to call for a booking, do so. If your tape is rejected, don't be upset. Not everyone is going to love your act, and reasons other than quality of material may have caused the rejection. You may be a comic musician and the booker already has several comic musicians on the roster. Whatever the case, most bookers will give you feedback about your act if asked.

77

And, after a period of time, most bookers will look at another tape. A work of caution: If you send a second tape be sure the material is significantly different. Bookers keep notes on audition tapes. If you get a second chance, be grateful and send a different tape.

When you send the videotape, remember that this is an audition. You have asked the booker to watch your tape, not the other way around. An audition should be a representation of the kind of work you can do. If you send a tape and later tell the booker that the tape was old and you have funnier stuff now, you have wasted everyone's time and money. Bookers' only acquaintance with you is through that tape. They see only what has been recorded. They do not see the difficulties you had to overcome to make the tape. They may be able to see that you have potential, but they will not book you on potential. They will only see, and buy, the show itself.

Because you have requested the audition, send a return envelope with postage along with the tape; otherwise do not expect it to be returned.

One last thought: Several years ago it was acceptable for a comic to send either an audiotape or a videotape. The audiotape is no longer an option. Stand-up comedy is a visual craft, and the videotape is the only medium that captures it for auditions. If you are also a musician and have an album on audiotape, send it along with your videotape as an extra perk. However, don't expect an audiotape of music to clinch a booking in a comedy club.

KEEPING RECORDS

As a stand-up comedian, you are a small business. Like any other business you must make a routine of keeping records and dealing with items like income, outgo, and taxes. The habits you form at this stage of your career will stay with you. Make your bookkeeping procedures methodical, and you can avoid costly mistakes.

Taxes. Like it or not you will have to pay taxes as a stand-up comedian. How much tax you pay and when must be worked out with an accountant who has experience with entertainers. To find such a person, you can ask another entertainer for a referral or call accountants and ask if they know anything about entertainment law. When you have found the right person, he or she will tell you what kind of receipts to keep and what you can legally deduct. This is another good use for your journal—keeping track of mileage, job-related expenses, etc. Do what your accountant says, but always keep an eye on your own finances. Too often we read about entertainers who have turned their finances over to another only to be hit with big lawsuits or back taxes because certain payments weren't made. Just because recordkeeping can be boring and you're into being funny and creative doesn't mean that you can ignore it.

The nightclubs you work for will consider you an independent contractor. Independent contractors are not employees of the club. The employer (the club) controls only the result of your work, not the means and method of accomplishing that result. As an independent contractor, taxes are not withheld from your check. Instead, you will be given your payment in a lump sum and asked to fill out a W-9 (Request for Taxpayer Identification Number and Certification) or an in-house independent contractor form. Both of these documents call for your full, real name, address, phone, and social security number. At the end of the club's fiscal year, if they have paid you $600 or more, you will be sent a form 1099 notifying you that the venue has reported to the IRS paying you a certain amount of money. Save all these 1099s and give them to your accountant at tax time. If you have kept up with your journal and saved receipts, taxes should be fairly easy (and less expensive) to prepare.

NECESSARY SUPPLIES

You must have guessed by now that you will have to invest some money into getting your career off the ground. You have paid for pictures, resumes or bios, and video tapes. What next? The following are items you can buy in bulk and should keep on hand: postage, videotape-size padded mailing envelopes, 9 × 12 manila mailing envelopes, strapping tape, good marking pen, material or idea journal, and a comprehensive datebook.

The padded mailing envelopes can be stamped and stuffed with the videotape you are sending in the 9 × 12 manila envelope. Be sure to fill out all the address information on both envelopes. These envelopes can be bought by the dozen at office supply houses or off-price clubs. Buy them in bulk and save money. The padded envelopes will protect your videotapes and give you more use per tape. Plain or even fiberglass mailing envelopes are not enough protection for tapes sent by regular mail.

The comprehensive datebook should be of the type with lots of compartments and entry areas. Some features to look for are a month-to-month overview calendar, a two-year day-to-day calendar, an expandable phone and address section, a mileage journal, an expense section, receipt pouches, and enough room to add extra note sheets. Many of these datebooks are expensive initially, some over $150. However, the major expense is for the cover and some of the indexes. After the first year, all you pay for are the dated inserts. It is worth the investment, as a good notebook will last for years.

Still want to be a comic? Think things over. Up to

Billy Crystal hosts the 64th Annual Academy Awards.

now the investment has been principally emotional. The time has come to match that investment financially. If you're still willing and have a day job that will allow you to travel—read on.

8

Life on the Road

It is a foregone conclusion that comedians who wish to broaden their career have to leave home base and go on the road. Even if there are a dozen or more local clubs that pay beginning comics, you still need to branch out into other markets to begin building your strength. Just as a club attracts a certain kind of audience, cities, in general, do the same thing. Most experienced bookers can look at comics and see Chicago or San Francisco or Houston in their performance. What they see has nothing to do with accent or dress, but rather attitude, level of material—style. A comic who has tons of funny, but regional, material will have trouble getting booked outside a specific geographical area. To be able to play to all kinds of markets, your material needs to appeal to a wide variety of audiences. The only way to expand your material horizons is to go on the road. Start small, and travel only short distances at first. You may not yet be ready to leave the state, but you definitely need to leave town to expand your career.

The types of clubs that book young, beginning

comedians for money share some characteristics. The club usually has an overall low budget; it is not a four-star establishment; its technical equipment is minimal; and its staff is not experienced in comprehensive comedy club management. This is not to say that the audience and the ambiance won't be great—just that you will be walking into comedy on a shoestring.

In most cases, you go from job to job by using your car or riding in another comic's car. If your car is being used and someone is riding with you, it is perfectly reasonable to expect some gas money from the rider, and vice versa. At any rate, you should keep your car in good working order. Many small rooms are not in metropolitan areas, and you don't want to be stuck out in the boonies late at night with car trouble. It is a good idea to join an auto club that provides emergency road service. A club less than three hours from home base will probably not offer lodging, so plan to return home the same evening.

If the club is more than three hours from home base, some travel money may be offered, or you can request gas money. The club may even have an allowance to cover round-trip air fare. If such an allowance is offered, the club will reimburse you from your ticket. The club may have an in-house system for ground transfer from the airport. Be sure to ask about it. If the club has no system, you may need to take a bus or hotel shuttle. When a club offers an air allowance and is more than three hours from home base, lodging is usually part of the offer. It is your responsibility to get all the information necessary to fulfill a booking. Know where you are to be, what time you are to go on, where you are staying, how much you will be paid, and what are the travel arrangements. Make a list of questions to be answered by the booker, and go through your checklist with each booking.

ACCOMMODATIONS ON THE ROAD

Many comedy clubs are in hotels. Sometimes they are designated rooms that do only comedy. Sometimes they are lounges that have different kinds of entertainment, comedy being just one or two nights. These clubs will house you at the hotel, covering charges for a single room and tax. Additional services such as room service, dry cleaning, phone calls, and movies are the responsibility of the comic. The room is covered only for the night or nights that you work. If you wish to stay for additional nights, the hotel may have a discount rate for employees; if such a rate exists, take advantage of it.

Other comedy clubs are freestanding. They may be bars or lounges doing comedy as part of an entertainment schedule, or full-time rooms. Accommodations for the freestanding rooms vary. Some clubs will house you in a nearby hotel or motel, in which case the venue pays only room and tax for the nights you work.

Other clubs lease an apartment or condo to house their talent, usually a two- or three-bedroom housekeeping apartment. These facilities are usually equipped with linens, cooking utensils, dishes, silverware, towels, and at least weekly maid service. This allows you to prepare some of your own meals and save money on a week-long booking. The condo arrangements have a definite pecking order. The headliner rates the master bedroom and usually a private bath. If a rental car is offered, the headliner controls the keys. The feature act and the opening act usually share a bath and sometimes a bedroom. (Not to worry, you won't have to share a bed.) Most club owners make every effort to give you a private room, no matter what your place in the lineup. If you are part of a duo or team act, you are considered a single act for all intents and purposes. Your lodging, travel allowance, and talent fee are divided by the number of people in the act. Clubs work on very tight budgets, especially for the opening and/or feature act. If they pay a feature $500 per week, that is what they will offer your duo or team. For this reason, it is rare to see teams working the road

Ups and Downs of the Road

Time to do another comedy reality check. Traveling, especially by car, can be interesting and provide lots of new material. It can also be very tedious. If long car trips make you ill or uncomfortable, comedy may not be right for you. Don't kid yourself, there will be no way to avoid driving to engagements during the first third or so of your career—and maybe longer. That means a lot of hours driving alone or with someone you don't know very well. At your destination, you will be in still another hotel or motel for a short stay; or in another condo for a short stay; or in another comedy club that looks familiar but has a whole new type of audience for you to figure out. You will most certainly be living out of a suitcase, and after a while you will experience disorientation in not having familiar things about you. Even if you are traveling only on weekends, your relationships will take on a long-distance aspect.

You will literally be working all the time at first: working at your job or at school during the week, and as a comic in the evenings, on weekends, or both. Time to go to the movies, to grocery shop, do yard work, or pick up the dry cleaning is at a premium. Things that you always used to stay on top of start to slide. Planning and time budgeting become a big issue. It will seem that everyone wants a piece of you and there's not enough to go around. Your focus and desire to make it in comedy may not be shared by significant others. If you have defined personal commitments, now is the time to evaluate whether or not you can maintain them. If you are a newlywed, a parent, or a primary caregiver for someone, traveling may be out of the question, which means that comedy is out of the question. If your family does not support your efforts, it will be difficult for you to concentrate on improving. Sit down with the people in your life and explain as best you can what is required of you right now. Try to map out potential scheduling problems, foreseeable financial problems, and points that might become emotionally straining. Try to eliminate the surprises for your loved ones. It will make life much easier in the long run.

To keep everything in sync, you need a pervasive positive attitude. See your goal and keep reaching for it. If you get down on yourself, the game is lost. Put yourself in a position to go forward in comedy. If you have a day job, make sure it allows you to travel or at least leave on short notice. Keep your overall schedule flexible. If you are naturally shy, start trying to become a "people person." You may quite often share lodging with a complete stranger; work at finding ways of enjoying this situation. It is a hard and fast rule of the business that personal problems you don't deal with eventually show up on the stage. A good comic turns tragedy into a useful piece of the act. A red flag should go up when you find yourself using the stage to air personal complaints or philosophies (that don't have a punchline). The bitter comic is often the comic on his or her way out rather than up.

AN INTERVIEW WITH DAVID DANIEL

Like most comedians (and show business people in general), David Daniel won't tell you his real age. He looks, like most comedians (and show business people in general), much younger than he really is. With a choir-boy face and devilish blue eyes, his slight California drawl targets him as a native. David looks like the definitive surfer dude complete with shoulder-length

DAVID DANIEL

blond hair. He begins his act by turning his back to the audience and saying, "Guys, have you ever been driving down the road, see this long hair in the car in front of you, pull up next to it, smile, AND SHE'S A HE? I'm that guy." Then an agent suggested that he cut his hair and look more mainstream. He got the haircut but left the agent. The jury appears to be still out as to whether or not he's comfortable with this mainstream hair.

Like most comics today, David Daniel is not a household name—at least, not yet. He is, like most working comics today, a road comic. He travels by car from city to city all over the country, working about forty to forty-nine weeks out of the year. In most of the clubs David plays, he performs in the middle or headline position. He would prefer to headline in all of them (any comic would), but he sometimes has to take middle slots just to keep working.

The following interview was conducted by phone: I was in Houston, and David was in South Dakota.

Q: Tell me, briefly, about yourself.

A: I grew up in California. L.A. Spent my summers surfing. Love to surf. I went to college, San Diego State University, got a BA, then went to West Virginia University and got an MA and a PhD in psychology.

Q: So you're a doctor?

A: I'm a doctor.

Q: You're a doctor, but you make your living as a stand-up comedian. What's the story?

A: I was living in LA. Surfing and in college. LOVE TO SURF. One night I wandered into The Comedy Store [landmark Los Angeles comedy club]. I watched for a while, and then I got rowdy. I started smarting off to the guys on stage. This one comic, who is now my friend, pulled me aside and said if I was going to try to be funny, why didn't I go on stage. I'm sure he meant that as a put-down to shut me up, but I didn't take it that way. I decided to give it a try. So I went home, worked on some stuff, went to open-mic night, bombed at first, kept trying and kept trying. Performing stand-up got into my blood. It became as necessary to me as surfing and other—necessary stuff. Then I got accepted at graduate school. I was really torn. Did I want to continue college or keep after comedy? I eventually did both: I went to school and did comedy on the weekends. It was a much better part-time job than working in food service. When I got out of graduate school I decided that stand-up was what I really wanted to do. If I don't make it I can still buy a couch, but I know I'm going to [make it].

Q: Do you now or have you ever practiced psychology professionally?

A: I volunteer as a psychologist on a Sioux reservation in South Dakota. I go there several times a year and help out. It's an incredibly spiritual place. You feel it just walking around.

Q: How long have you been doing comedy?

A: Six, almost seven years.

Q: What was the best job you've had in comedy, so far?

A: The best job is almost always my latest job. Every time I go up I think this is going to be a "magic night." You know, that night when everything works—I mean everything. And you try some new material and that works. Everything. I always go up thinking that will happen.

Q: Does it?

A: Yeah, but only about two times a year. Really. But put that in perspective. How many times in life do things work out perfectly? Never, right? If I have a magic night twice a year, then I'm beating the odds. There was this one night in LA. I was at the Laff Factory and Rodney Dangerfield had just gone up and killed. The back-stage guy told me I was supposed to follow Rodney, and I thought . . . well, you know what I thought. That I was going to suck and everyone would hate me after Dangerfield—I mean the guy's a freaking legend. So I go up and things are good, then better, then great. I killed too! That would have to be an extra special magic night.

Q: What was the worst job you've had in comedy, so far?

A: Man—in Tennessee. I'm not going to say the name of the club—who knows, they might hire me back some day. Anyway, I'm doing my show and things are—OK, not great, not terrible. That was during that time when David Duke and the Klan were in the news a lot. like to do topical material, and I'd written this bit earlier that afternoon and—well, I figured I was OK to try some new stuff. So I told this anti-Klan joke. I don't even remember the joke now. Anyway, this guy in the audience stood up and pulled a gun on me. He definitely didn't like the anti-Klan material.

Q: What did you do?

A: I got out of there. I ended my set and got the hell out of Dodge. I may love performing but I'm not a fool—I mean I've got a PhD.

Q: You are a road comic?

Comedian Richard Pryor.

A: Right.
Q: You're in a different city every week. Sometimes a different city every night. What do you
do when you're not performing?
A: Mostly I write and drive. I mean, I am a road

91

comic. I spend a whole lot of time in my car by myself. I drive and I make verbal notes for material. I drive and I eat. I drive and drive and drive. I know every trick of the road, every good place to stop, everything there is to know about driving. When I get to where I'm supposed to be that day, I like to get out and walk and look at the different things and talk to people. I learn things about people and from people. Then I try to put in about three hours' writing time a day. Mostly I do that after the shows.

Q: Do you ever rely on your experiences as a psychologist to develop material?

A: Sure. I sometimes handle crowds the way you would this real big, noisy therapy group. I bond with the group and try and draw them in and trust me to entertain them. I have this bit, "I used to take my therapy patients on field trips. I'd take the guys with castration anxieties to weeny roasts on the weekends. Then I'd take all the women with oral fixations to my house."

9

Who Hires Comedians?

Talent is brought to a comedy club through the efforts of a person designated as the club's booking agent. Basically, the three types of comedy club booking agents are the in-house agent, the independent agency, and the club owner. Let's take a closer look at these three types of bookers.

THE IN-HOUSE AGENT

The in-house agent is an employee of the comedy club and, more than likely, a resident of the city where the club is located. Working for one club, he or she probably books only rooms that are owned or sanctioned by the employing club. This person can negotiate fees within the parameters set by an immediate superior, the club owner. Any variation from the fee schedule requires an OK by the owner. Usually the in-house booker performs some other function, perhaps marketing director, day or night manager, or bar manager. Any one of these jobs would involve day and night hours, something quite common in bar management. The reasons for the dual functions are that (a) booking talent is not very time-consuming for only one or two rooms; and (b) a person who works both day and night has an opportunity to see firsthand the crowd response to a comic he or she has booked. In-house bookers tend to be new to the comedy business, attracted, like the comedians themselves, to a fun business. As they mature in their job, they become very good at picking talent for their particular room. They see what appeals to their audiences and book accordingly.

This impacts the comedian in a number of ways. In-house bookers will bring popular acts back more often than those who work for several venues. They will headline an act that is successful in their room faster than bookers working for other venues. Traditionally they do not audition as many comics as other bookers, so their choice and taste can be limited. In-house bookers are more likely to agree to a piggyback booking from a favorite act than a booker for a number of venues. They will not be as concerned with your position in the lineup in other clubs as, say, the agency booker or the club owner. If you are used to opening but the in-house booker feels that your act is popular enough to middle or headline, you will be offered the higher slot.

The caution here is that bookers working for several venues may not move you up the roster with similar speed. It will be much harder to move up the ladder with the agency booker than the in-house booker. Telling the agency booker that, "Mary Smith from Comedy Club, Anywhere USA uses me as a headliner," will do little to advance your cause. The booker knows exactly why you are headlined so quickly at that room: Your act has connected well with the audiences in *one* room. That doesn't mean you have the maturity to do so in larger, more sophisticated rooms.

When you are engaged by an in-house booker, more than likely no commission will be due. The salary of the booker is paid by the club. As with all booking agents, however, it is politically a good idea to ask if a commission is due.

THE BOOKING AGENT

The independent booking agency is usually a freestanding business contracting its services to venues that want comics. These agencies usually have exclusive contracts with the venues; they alone provide talent for the clubs. It would be counterproductive for an agency to be scheduling talent for a room in competition with another agency. Independent booking agencies work for a number of venues. They do not, if they are reputable, book two establishments in the same city, which would be a serious conflict of interest. These agencies do, however, book private functions in the same city with no ethical breach. The rationale is that a private function is a one-time-only collection of people with a common interest; such an event is not in direct competition with their contract club. Events that fall under this "private function" category would be conventions, private parties, trade shows, tournaments, award ceremonies, fundraisers, colleges, etc. Comedians booked into a comedy club in a city may also work such special events with no conflict of interest. It is the rule, however, that bookings into special events may never interfere with the club schedule. Also, any publicity that may be gleaned from the special booking should be directed toward the comedy club. For instance, "Comedian John Doe, after dinner entertainment for the Rotary, may be seen at Comedy Club, Anywhere, USA, May 10–15." It is definitely not a good idea to book yourself into competing rooms back to back; you may end up losing both rooms for future bookings. If you have any doubt about booking conflicts in a city, consult the booker or the club owner.

Independent booking agencies usually book several

rooms at the same time. These rooms fall into a "circuit" creating anywhere from a week to many weeks of work for the comic. If you do well under a variety of circumstances, bookers may offer you something with all the clubs they book. If you are not consistent or work only for a certain type of audience, they will limit what they offer you. Some bookers have so many clubs that the comic may actually decline work to retain the opportunity to play for other employers. Some bookers have very small circuits, representing only a week or two of work. These engagements should be treated with the same respect and professionalism as the larger ones. You never know in this business who will be able to help if you have a sudden dropout or cancellation.

The independent booking agency ordinarily provides the comedy club with promotional materials on comedians, executed contracts, and advance schedules (complete with fees) and handles any comic-related problems. The agent also negotiates and provides support for celebrity concerts commissioned by the club client; all the venue has to do is keep the doors open and the club staffed. The agent is one-stop shopping for the venue, responsible for the success or failure of the comics booked. If there is any kind of problem with the comic, the venue calls the booker to solve it. Such problems vary, but the most common seem to be failure to provide promotional materials when requested; showing up at the club late or unable to work; confusion about fees, travel or lodging benefits, or show times; replacement for cancellations; missed promotional appearances, and personality conflicts with the club staff. Most booking agencies do everything they can to avoid on-site problems. They send letters of confirmation, information sheets, and/or contracts to the talent in an attempt to avoid mix-ups. Promotional materials not received in time may result in cancellation of the talent.

Promotional appearances "missed" by the talent may result in a pay deduction. Other problems may result in the talent's not being booked back into that venue. Despite all precautions, however, problems still happen, and the booking agent has to be on call to handle them.

Independent booking agents are paid in various ways. Some charge the contract club a weekly fee. Some charge a weekly fee and a small percentage from the talent. Some clubs pay their bookers for everything—talent fees, travel fees, booking fees. The agents then pay the talent and do the tax work at the end of the year. Some agents take no fee from the venue, but do take a percentage from the talent. Be sure to ask about the commission schedule of an agent who offers you a job. If you accept the job, you accept the commission schedule, so be prepared to pay it.

THE CLUB OWNER

The third variety of booking agent is the club owner, a person who books talent for rooms that he or she owns. Club owners are the final word when it comes to booking, for obvious reasons. If you do well in their room, they will have you back; if you don't, they won't. Club owners rarely give second chances. They are the ones least likely to believe that you were just having an "off week" when you did poorly. They are the least likely to accept excuses for a missing this or a late that. You are a direct conduit to their livelihood. If you fail and the audiences slack off for a week, there is every likelihood that they will see no income that week. They are, and should be, highly selective about who and what appears on their stage. Club owner/bookers are inclined to bring comics back only so long as there is audience request and the fees don't increase dramatically. Comics who raise their fees with each appearance may soon find the club owner unwilling to rebook. If one comic can be developed into a "star" in their room, so can others. Why not start over with a fresh (and less expensive) face? With so many comedians working and so many with similar styles, it is relatively easy to replace an expensive comic with an inexpensive clone. That may not be fair, but it's the way things are for club owners.

Club owner/bookers usually do not charge commissions. Their money comes from a good return at the bar and box office. But again, out of courtesy, ask if a commission is due on the engagement.

ROLE OF THE BOOKING AGENT

Regardless of who is doing the booking, certain conditions exist for the person hiring the talent. Their primary function is to keep a constant flow of good talent into the club. They cannot afford to engage a month of nationally known comics followed by a month of no-credit comics. This sort of overbooking will make the quality of the club seem irregular, and attendance will be good only when the recognizable name is booked. The increased talent fees for the celebrity comic will make these bookings prohibitive, and the club will fall into a pattern of feast or famine, which is unhealthy financially. Nor can the club afford to underbook the room, routinely booking cheap acts that are either inexperienced for their slot in the lineup or no good. An opening act working the headline slot for opening-act pay still may only have opening quality. Comedians are usually so eager to say that they "headlined" a room that they forget about being able to pull the job off. Weeks of "ho-hum" comics produces similar income for the club. Ideally, the booker maintains as much variety and as many levels of talent as the room will bear. The room becomes the star, rather than the comic. People come to the club because they know something funny is always going on there. They are confident that the quality of entertainment will be consistent from week to week. With this kind of cycle, there is every reason to expect that the club will become a solid, vigorous business.

Another universal function of the booking agent is to negotiate the lowest possible talent fee for the club. Don't be alarmed when this happens to you—it's part of the booker's job. Most booking agents (even club owners) have a set budget for talent and travel, and their goal is to go under this figure. They most certainly will not go over it unless you are a celebrity, you are likely to recoup the increase in revenue, or there is some other factor that will recover the increased fees such as a convention or private parties. If you ask for a rebooking, they will look at the business you did on your last visit; any fee increase will be based on that. If this is your first booking with a club, expect to come in at the bottom of the pay scale. If you do well, there will be someplace for you to go financially with the organization.

Last, but not least, bookers screen talent by the tools discussed in Chapter 7. They primarily audition through videotapes, then live auditions or "showcases"; cable, TV, or other broadcast mediums using stand-up comedians; recommendations from other club owners or bookers, and recommendations from trusted comedians. No matter what audition tool you choose, remember that this is an audition. This is a try-out. This is a chance for a stranger to see you practice your craft. As a general rule, the auditioner knows nothing about your act. The tape is the all-inclusive "it." The viewer will not believe you are funny if your tape is not; not believe you have a solid twenty minutes if it isn't on there; and not be impressed with original material if it doesn't exist

Three of "The Not Ready for Prime Time Players," Gilda Radner, Bill Murray, and Jane Curtin, in a "Nerds" segment on "Saturday Night Live."

on the tape. Make the tape something you are proud of and can send with confidence.

FINDING BOOKERS

The easiest way for young comics to find out who is booking what is to ask another comedian. Other comics will be able to tell you not only who the booker is, but what kind of engagement (including money) is involved in the booking. Keep your all-purpose datebook with you so you can note new information when you come across it. If you are in the habit of writing notes to yourself on napkins or scraps of paper, remember to transfer them to your datebook at the earliest possible moment. A good contact can be lost if you stuff a phone number in your pocket and then forget who it belongs to.

Another way of finding bookers is to call clubs you would like to play and ask who books the room and what is the booking process. Submit the materials or call for an audition as directed, and you can save not only time but long-distance calls.

Some comics find leads for both clubs and club booking agents through professional publications. *Just for Laughs* is a monthly newspaper distributed free in comedy clubs. Mail subscriptions are also available. *JFL* has a regular section called "On the Road," which lists comedy clubs, addresses (no zip), and phone numbers by state. It also lists who is playing where and the date of the booking if supplied by the venue. As you begin to know your fellow comics, reading a lineup will give you an idea of the kind of talent a club books and the talent fees involved.

Comedy USA Industry Guide is a magazine-size book printed yearly by Comedy USA. It is a detailed guide listing not only comedy clubs but comics, agents, managers, writers, TV and cable production companies,

101

cruise bookers, competitions, other publications, charities, festivals, and more. There is a one-time fee for this publication. For information, write to P.O. Box 20214, New York, NY 10028.

Another source of booking information is the Professional Comedians Association, or PCA, which defines itself as follows: "The PCA is an organization of comedians that was formed to support the interests and well-being of its members and to enhance their professional and economic standing." The PCA is not a labor union. It sells memberships to qualified comedians and associate memberships to other industry professionals. Members receive an industry guide of comedy clubs, including information on working conditions, the opportunity to buy into insurance plans, and rental discounts. For information on membership, write to 581 Ninth Avenue, New York, NY 10036.

A couple of final thoughts on finding a booker: Never throw away a phone number. Keep numbers in your book (with notes if possible); don't white them out because a club has closed or the agent has moved on. People in this business tend to disappear and then resurface. It can be very helpful in your search for work to "find" a person you knew from one venue now working for another. If you have had a positive relationship with that person in the past, the whole audition process may be waived in the new room. Be nice to everyone. Bridge-burning is for arsonists, not comedians.

Tracking down a booking agent is still another opportunity for you to practice patience. Remember, while you are calling, trying to get work, trying to speak to the agent: Hundreds of other comics are doing the same thing. Persons who book popular rooms get dozens of calls from comics *a day*. After a while (a very little while), they get tired of the calls. They are "out" more than they are "in." Someone screens their calls. They can be elusive to the point of being frustrating. They may tell you to call at a certain time and not be there when you do. Don't take any of this personally; it's not directed at you. There are only so many jobs to go around, and bookers can get discouraged telling good people that they have no work. Keep trying and keep smiling.

10

How Much Does It Pay?

One of the questions a booker is asked most often, right after "Can I have a job," is "How much does it pay?" Pay scales, like a lot of things in show business, are not always what they seem. We can all read in the papers that Bill Cosby gets mega millions a year and Michael Jackson made a zillion on this and a zillion on that. It does not necessarily track, however, that everyone in show business makes a ton of dough. The Screen Actors Guild reports regularly that the bulk of the money going to Guild members is made by less than 10 percent of the membership.

As has been mentioned, talent in stand-up comedy is paid either by the show or by percentage based on what the box office will sell.

BY THE SHOW
If you are paid by the show, six things go into determining your fee:

- Number of shows
- Position in the lineup
- Number of nights

- Perks such as travel and lodging
- Size of the room
- Geographical location

A club booking two comics—a headliner and a feature —for one show, one night in a nonmajor market location (not extreme East or West coast) generally offers between $125 and $175 per show for the feature act and between $175 and $250 per show for the headline act, plus lodging and sometimes a travel allowance. If a second show is added on that one night, talent fees do not necessarily double, but probably increase by at least half.

For the same comics in the same location, for a multiple-night, multiple-show week, the club will generally offer between $500 and $700 per week to the feature and between $900 and $1,500 per week to the headliner. In addition, the club should provide lodging and sometimes a travel allowance. These figures are based on a six- or seven-show week at the same location.

Don't start waving these figures in front of club owners saying, "Hey, how come I'm not making what it says here?" Talent fees vary tremendously from one part of the country to another. They also vary based on the type of room you are playing and your actual credits. You may be offered low money in a room that normally pays on the high end because you are a beginner. The variables in pay scales can go on forever, and there is no national regulation of pay scales similar to those found in performing unions. Again, the rule is, there aren't any rules.

Whatever the pay, if you can't live with it when it is offered, turn it down and look for another job. The very worst thing you can do is accept a job, have second thoughts, then call back and cancel because the pay is too low. If you make the commitment to work for five bucks—do the job, and remember the next time that five bucks isn't good enough.

BY PERCENTAGES

If you are paid by percentage, this is how the math is done.

1. Take the number of shows times the number of seats times the average ticket price and arrive at the GP, or Gross Potential. Here's an example:

A club owner wants you to do four shows in a 200-seat house and is going to charge $5 per ticket per show.

$$200 \times 4 = 800 \times \$5 = \$4,000.$$

Thus, $4,000 is the GP on the box office if the club owner sells every seat for every show.

2. Take the GP and figure the sales tax in that state. Here's an example:

The sales tax is 5 percent of each ticket. Multiply $4,000 by 5 to get the sales tax on the GP.

$$\$4,000 \times .05 = \$200$$

Subtract $200 from the $4,000 for an adjusted GP, or AGP. (All venues make offers based on what money will be available at a sell-out after taxes. They have to pay tax on the tickets and do not consider that money as working capital.)

The AGP is now $3,800. From that $3,800 the club owner must also pay travel, lodging (if the show is not in a hotel), and advertising. The venue will keep subtracting at this point in round numbers:

AGP $3,800 − $250 travel − $1,000 advertising
　　　　　　　　　　　　　− $150 lodging = $2,400

3. The venue will now offer a deal based on the knowledge that, if they sell all the tickets, the most they can make at the box office is $2,400. Of course, they will make additional money if there is a bar and/or food service. But while food and beverage are lucrative they are not pure profit. They have their own equations for determining profit and are not dealt with here.

The offer, then, will come in this form: a guarantee vs. a percentage of the box office, whichever is greater. With the figures above, the offer might be $1,200 vs. 80 percent of the door, after taxes, whichever is greater. This means you would receive $1,200 no matter what. If you sell out, you could receive up to $1,900 plus expenses.

Percentage offers are generally reserved for celebrity comics going into a large venue for a limited run. They are usually not viable for either the comic or the club on a smaller scale. There are, however, clubs that offer to split a percentage of the box office with the comic in lieu of a flat fee. Go into such an offer with your eyes open. If you agree to a percentage of box office, know what the percentage of complimentary tickets and discounted tickets will be and get some idea of the cost of promotion. Also, be there when the tickets (and money) are counted. Many a young comic has been burned in a deal like this, where the house was full but the owner says everyone was comped and there is no money to split.

11

Talent Representation

Talent representation can seem like a confusing web of people and job titles to the stand-up comedian. That's because it *is* a confusing web of people and job titles. No standard job descriptions are adhered to by the people who make a living representing live performers. They usually define their own boundaries based on how they want to pursue an income. Some states define "manager" and "agent" in an attempt to regulate their activities and tax their income; but these controls vary geographically. The following is an attempt to explain representation as it applies to the stand-up comedian.

The first distinction is between club bookers, agents, and managers. Club bookers are responsible for hiring comics. They are advocates for the *venue*, always negotiating in the favor of the venue. They "represent" the venue to comedians. Agents are responsible for finding work for the comic. They are advocates for the *talent*, always seeking better money, perks, etc. for the performer. They "represent" the artist to the venue. Managers also are advocates for the talent, working with bookers and agents to promote the career of their client.

TALENT AGENT

The talent agent seeks work for the artist. Talent agents work by themselves or in a group. In a one-person agency, the owner of the business calls all the shots. This person may employ an assistant or subagent to type contracts, give out information, and perform clerical duties. The subagent may not negotiate fees or guarantee jobs unless directed to do so by the agent. The agency with several agents employs several people to work in the same capacity. Whatever the size of the agency, its basic function is to take and solicit work for the artist. Talent agencies represent many artists. Commissions are their only source of income. The commission the talent agent receives can come from the talent, the talent buyer, or both.

Does the beginning stand-up comedian need a talent agent? Yes and no. Yes, if you want to do stand-up and audition for radio, TV cable, feature film, or industrial film. Yes, if you live in an area (like New York) that has lots of professional live theater. Under these conditions, you need an exclusive arrangement with a talent agent. Without the agent, you will not find out about auditions.

No, you do not need a talent agent for club work. Beginning comics need to build personal relationships with club owners and bookers. To begin this relationship, one must first make a booking call. Making your own booking calls, negotiating your own fees, and finding out about the club requirements is a good way to learn the business and meet new people. Beginning comics who ask a friend or significant other to call a booker and pose as an agent appear silly and amateurish to the booker.

Nonetheless, there are some important things any young performer should know about talent agents. The title "talent agent" can easily be maneuvered to serve the purposes of swindlers. Con artists dangle the glitter of show business in front of the starry-eyed, taking the victim on a long, expensive ride. Some states require talent agents to be licensed in an attempt to eliminate the charlatans; some don't. There are, however, certain things that reputable talent agents do and don't do. Knowing them should give inexperienced entertainers an idea of the kind of talent agent or agency they are confronting.

- Reputable talent agents are franchised by one or more of the professional performing unions: Equity (Actor's Equity Association, the union for stage actors); AFTRA (American Federation of Television and Radio Artists, the union for radio, TV, and industrial film actors); SAG (Screen Actors Guild, the union for feature film, industrial film, cable, and TV actors); and AGVA (American Guild of Variety Artists, the union for variety artists, live performances). Being franchised by one or more unions means that the talent agency complies with union standards to insure health, safety, and proper compensation for the artist. Unions, after contract negotiations with agents and producers, set the amount of commission an agent can charge on a job performed under a union contract. Unions also determine the "scale" or minimum amount a performer can be paid for a particular job when performed under the appropriate union contract. Commissions on union jobs are billed in addition to the performers' pay so that the artists never receive less than the base scale fee negotiated by the agent for the job. The artist may receive more money than the base scale amount, but never less.
- Reputable talent agents *do not* charge for representation. Agents receive a commission after

you have been hired and paid for a job. Reputable agents *do not* charge a "setup" fee or "listing" fee. Reputable agents *do not* list you without charge and then require you to pay for classes or photos before being sent on auditions. Reputable talent agents do not charge for auditions.

- Reputable agents *do* have the option of listing or not listing you with their agency. Even large agencies with lots of calls will take only so many "short guys with bald heads" or "mommy-teacher-secretary" looks. Most reputable talent agents put together a composite video or voice tape featuring their talent. They use this tape as a selling tool to producers. These master tapes are usually produced once a year. The agent may offer you the opportunity to be featured on the tape. You may accept or decline this offer without being dropped from the agency roster. The agent does charge a flat fee for participation in the master tape; the fees pay for the production and distribution. The agent does not make a profit on the fees and does not list them as income. Reputable agents may list you but suggest that you need new publicity photos or tapes. They usually have a list of photographers, studios, and technicians that they encourage you to use. The agent does not get a kickback from these people. They recommend these people because they produce good work and are reasonably priced. If you cannot afford new materials, discuss this with the agent; the reputable ones will work with you. Good agents know that young performers are always on a budget, and they are sympathetic.
- Reputable talent agents *do* tell you in advance of a job what your talent payment and the commission will be. If you are working under a union con-

111

tract, the agent's commission will automatically be a set fee on top of the producer's payment. If you are not working under a union contract, the reputable talent agent will tell you one of two things: You will receive a fee *plus* commission or a fee *less* commission. If you receive a fee plus commission, the producer is paying the agent's commission and the total talent fee comes to you. If the job is a fee less commission, the agent's commission is subtracted from your talent fee. Ask the agent what the commission percentage is before you accept the job. Once you have accepted the job, the commission, of whatever size, is due to the agent. If a producer books a job through a talent agent, full payment is usually issued to the agency. The reputable agency should pay you no later than three days after receiving the producer's check (to allow it to clear the bank), subtracting the appropriate fees. The reputable talent agent will issue your 1099 at the end of the year for jobs paid through their office.

Reputable talent agents *will* ask you to sign an exclusive contract. Such a contract can be detailed so that you can have an exclusive relationship with an agent for representation for film or radio or stage work, but not for work as a stand-up comic. Read any contract you are presented with and make changes as they apply to your career. Also, be sure to include an annual expiration date for your contract; in that way you avoid being "joined at the hip" to a person you may outgrow. Agents request exclusivity because they need to know the status of their roster when producers call. Agents invest time, effort, and money into developing talent for work in certain markets. They need something to bind you to them for a given period so they have time to recoup some of their investment.

PERSONAL MANAGER

Personal managers have a dozen or fewer artists on their roster. Their primary task is to help select and solicit work offers for their talent. Personal managers focus on long-term career guidance. They cover the entire industry for their artists, weighing offers from clubs, movie producers, concert promoters, and so on. Bookings are taken for purposes of career advancement as well as their dollar amount. In addition to career guidance, the personal manager sometimes handles all financial and business dealings for the client, from paying the light bill to buying real estate or investing. Many times the manager becomes a buffer between the artist and the real world. The degree of involvement in the artist's career and life is usually carefully constructed in a contract between the two.

Personal managers are paid like business consultants. They negotiate their own contracts to receive a set percentage from the artist's income. Their percentage is higher than that of the talent agent because their service is more comprehensive. The relationship between personal manager and artist is usually of longer duration than the talent agent's. The artist may change talent agents several times while retaining the same personal manager.

Do beginning comedians need personal managers? No. Managers are necessary only when the talent has gone as far as possible on his or her own. When contracts become complex and offers need to be evaluated, the talent needs a manager. Don't hire a manager before you have a career to manage. Young comics, eager to "have a manager," have been known to sign away much larger chunks of their income than is necessary or they

113

can afford. Even when there is a career to manage, it is never wise to hand your life over to the care of another. The newspapers too often report on celebrities who have lost everything because of misplaced trust in a manager. Accept the manager's advice, but don't do it blindly. Keep an overview of your career. Personal managers may schedule your life down to trips to the bathroom, but they are still employees. Business with its bank statements and tax payments may be boring, but the business of *your* career deserves *your* attention.

A type of representation that is fairly common among working comics is the **informal manager**. Road comics who are tired of the clerical work involved in their scheduling or want to break into a new circuit may develop an informal management relationship. These informal managers are usually people with other functions in the comedy biz. For example, a club booker who is trying to expand his or her business may "manage" comics in addition to booking them. This informal process may involve a verbal or sometimes written arrangement. The comic supplies the manager with all necessary promotional materials (tapes, photos, bio's, etc.) and tells the manager where he currently works. The manager is then free to solicit work for the comic in any new market. Sometimes the comic and the manager select new markets to be approached. Any new work or repeat bookings solicited for the comic under these conditions is subject to a commission. If a comic designates specific new markets with one manager, it is acceptable to have these informal relationships with a number of bookers or managers.

When working with several informal managers, be sure of the following: Keep the manager up-to-date on your whereabouts so that you can be reached to confirm a booking. Keep this person well supplied with promotional materials. Make sure two agents are not working on the same venue or market for you. You will be the loser if this happens. The club will not appreciate having several people call (sometimes with different prices) for the same comic. The manager who calls second and is told that someone has already contacted the club will feel foolish and appear to have poor communication with you. A manager who feels "used" will not continue to work for you and may drop you altogether.

Be sure to pay a commission for the job *each time* you are booked there. Pay the commission even if the club reschedules you personally, on site. Managers have no incentive to develop you in a new market if they only receive one payment while you receive several.

12

How to Make Booking Calls

All booking agents work differently, but a few areas are consistent within the profession. All booking agents set aside a time for scheduling comics. Some do a little bit weekly, some only on certain mornings, some every three months, and some as the spirit moves them. The trick for the comic is to find out when and to call at the right time. How do you get this information? Ask. If the agent is not booking when you call, ask when the next session will be. Some will give you a specific day and time; note this in your trusty date book/journal and call back then. Other bookers will give general time frames to allow themselves flexibility. It is not unusual to hear, "I'll try to start on the new year around the end of August." This tells you that their *intent* is to start scheduling for the new year during the last week of August. That may not happen; it's a goal. To call back on August 28 and insist that you were told you could be booked if you called on that date is incorrect. You may need to call several times to get to the booker when he or she *is* booking.

It is a given that it will be difficult to get through. Booking agents get dozens more calls than they have jobs to fill. They simply do not take all the calls. Don't be rude to people on the phone. One day they may have the booker's job and will remember bad manners.

What happens when you make call after call, follow all the rules, have patience to burn, and still can't get through to the booking agent? First, it is not a personal affront, so don't get angry and bitter. If it's happening to you, it's happening to others. The booker may have lost some rooms or have way too many calls for the number of jobs available. Give this booker a rest for several months and then try again.

"But I just want them to see my tape!" you say. Or, "The agent said he/she liked my tape and now I can't get booked!" Or, "I've already worked for this agent and done a good job. If I wait he/she'll forget about me." Sending your tape to a booking agent who is booked up for a year will not fill your calendar next month. Time is always on your side. Theoretically, your act will improve with time. A tape sent a year later than you planned will be stronger and perhaps yield more money. Better to send a tape when it will be well received than just have it watched and thrown onto a pile. Also, bookers cannot create openings where there are none. Good tapes and good jobs are not forgotten. Bookers routinely keep a card file on tapes they preview. They know who you are, when you sent the tape, and what their reactions were to your act. Bookers also send "report cards" to the clubs they book, requesting feedback about your engagement. When an opening occurs and you are on the other end of the line, the agent will refer to the report sheets to evaluate the possibility of another booking.

DON'TS AND DOS
Most booking agents are fairly flexible about taking calls from comics, but there are certain times *never* to call the

agent. It is hard enough to find work without phoning the agent at a bad time.

Never call a booking agent at home or outside of business hours unless specifically given permission. The booking agent is on twenty-four-hour call by the clubs, not the comics. Respect their privacy. If an agent gives you permission to call at home, make the conversation short and to the point. This is not a social call. There are several things *not* to ask during such conversation:

- "Who am I working with?" This is something you should have asked at the time of booking.
- "What are my flight plans?" Chances are the agent has sent you an information sheet detailing this information.
  "What am I getting paid in Podunk?" Clear this up at the time of booking.
- "Why won't you book me?" This is a business question—ask it during business hours.
- "Do you have any more work for me?" The agent's booking sheets are sure to be at the office.
- "Where do I go next week?" That is your problem, not the agent's. If you need to ask the question, call during business hours.
- "Where do I stay in Podunk?" Another question to be asked at the time of booking.
- "I'm in jail in Louisiana. Can you get me out?" The agent cannot smooth out all the bumps in your life. In fact, if you are in jail in Louisiana, the agent should be the last person you call!

Never call club owners/bookers during show times. True, they will be in the office, but not for booking purposes. While customers and staff are in the building, they must concentrate on the problems of the evening. Club owners/bookers are overseeing customer service, the waiter and bar staff, equipment, and entertainers. In any given night, something will go wrong with one or more of the above. It will be their responsibility to cope with the situation. They will not appreciate your call for work while they are taking care of business.

Never expect bookers to return your phone call, local or long distance. Even if they have a machine that says they will return all calls, it doesn't mean comics. The only time to expect agents to return calls is when they are trying to reach you. That may sound selfish, but consider their point of view. The average booking agent gets dozens of calls from comics each week; the cost in money and time would be prohibitive. Also, this is your call for work. You want a job, you should pay for the calls.

If you have reached the booking agent and have been given a job, there are several things you *should* ask at this point to make the engagement clear to you:

What is your position in the lineup? New comics are booked into a two-, three-, or four-person show. If it is a two-person show and you are starting out, chances are you will be booked as the feature act and will need about thirty to forty minutes of material. On a three-person show you could be either the open or the feature act. The feature needs about thirty minutes and the open about twenty minutes. The open will be asked to serve as MC for the other acts for no additional pay. On a four-person show, you will be either the MC or the open. The opening act needs twenty to thirty-five minutes of material, whereas the MC needs only enough to greet the crowd and bring up the other comedians. If you are the MC, you will be expected to know something about the other comics working the job.

The four-person and even three-person shows are

119

usually booked in 250-seat rooms. Any room smaller could not support that much talent. The average booking for a new comic is the two-person format.

What is your talent fee? Make sure you are told in advance exactly how much the job pays. Jobs that pay "around $300" may be closer to $200 when all is said and done.

Is a commission due? To whom? When? A very important question, this will affect your take-home pay and the income of the person doing the booking. If a commission is due, pay it as soon as you get your check. Delaying commission payments will influence how a booking agent schedules you in the future.

How many shows per engagement? The number of shows that clubs work per week varies dramatically. Weekend rooms may do only one show a night on Friday and Saturday, whereas full-week rooms do a total of four shows on the weekend. Find out in advance what the show requirement is, divide your after-commission pay by that number, and the quotient is your per-show pay. The pay will be fairly consistent with your slot in the lineup and the geographical location.

How long should each set be? Depending on your slot in the lineup and the number of comics on the bill, your show length will vary. Obviously, you will do more time on a two-person lineup than on a four-person lineup. The time factor can influence your pay: If you are on for fifteen minutes a show, you will be paid less than the person doing thirty minutes.

What are lodging provisions, if any? This is self-explanatory. Know whether and where the booking provides lodging. Try to arrange your travel so that you check in after 3 p.m. on the evening booked. If you are arriving later, call the hotel and make arrangements for late arrival.

What is the travel money, if any? Sometimes the

club pays for all travel to and from the venue; sometimes only a portion or an allowance is given. Some clubs allow the comic to purchase the airline ticket, with restrictions (21-day advance purchase), and reimburse the comic using the ticket as a receipt. Some clubs give you a flat amount, driving or flying. If the booking agent has sent you information on the travel procedures of the venue, read and heed it. If you fly, find out the club procedure on ground transfers. Taking a cab to a hotel from an airport can be almost as costly as the airline ticket. Ask about arrangements you can make for airport pickup. Some rooms have a designated staff person who picks up talent at the airport. Some rooms in hotels dispatch the hotel van. Whatever the procedure, know before you arrive. Whatever the travel allowance, the money is not intended as additional income for the comic. Clubs are very careful about reimbursement from receipts or tickets and feel put upon if the comic tries to make extra money on the deal. A comic who asks for air fare but intends to drive is considered to be taking advantage of the venue.

What additional promotional materials are needed by the booking agent or the club? Note in your datebook the number of pictures, etc. required and send them by the due date. Failure to send promotional materials when requested can result in cancellation. The easiest thing to do is keep a supply of photos and printed materials in your car, along with mailing envelopes, staples, etc.

Some booking agents make all their commitments over the phone, period. Others do a little more paperwork to secure the booking. If all you have is a telephone commitment, write down all the pertinent information and send it, with a return envelope, to the booker

COMEDY WORKSHOP PRODUCTIONS
2630 Fountainview
Houston, TX 77057
(713) 000–0000

Date

Dear

This letter is to confirm your booking with Comedy Club USA in Spirit Lake, Iowa. You are scheduled to perform in the headline position Tuesday-Saturday, on October 1–5, 1992. Talent fees due to you are $1200. Additional benefits due to you are lodging and a travel allowance of $250. Please consult the attached information sheet for specifics about this engagement.

Please send 10 promotional packets (with pictures) to the address listed above within 10 working days of receipt of this letter. Failure to supply requested promotional materials could result in cancellation.

The staff and management of Comedy Club USA look forward to your engagement. If you have questions regarding this booking that are not covered herein, please call Maurine Harker, Comedy Workshop Productions, at (713) 000–0000 Monday-Friday during working hours.

Sincerely,
Maurine Harker
Comedy Workshop Productions

Sample letter of confirmation.

COMEDY WORKSHOP PRODUCTIONS
2630 Fountainview
Houston, TX 77057
(713) 000–0000

Comedy Club USA is a new venue opening the first comedy club in the Spirit Lake area. This club will seat 250 and market toward 25–45-year-old professionals. The owner requests material kept in the PG-13 to R rating. Blue material is OK in moderation.

Club Name: Comedy Club USA

Club Address: XXXXXX, XXXXXXXX, Spirit Lake, Iowa 50158

Club Phone: (000) 000–000

Club Manager/contact: Marcie Rogers, Business Mgr., or John Borlan, Club Mgr.

Show Time: Tuesday-Saturday at 8:30 p.m.; additional shows on Friday and Saturday at 11:00 p.m. Call time is one hour prior to all acts.

Show Requirements: Headline: 50–60 min.; Feature: 30–40 min.; a house opening act will do 10–15 min. each night.

Lodging: All acts will be housed at the Holiday Arms, 123 Main, Spirit Lake, Iowa. (000) 000– 0000. Lodging is across the street from the club. Rooms will be listed under Comedy Club USA. Check-in is 3:00 p.m.; check-out, 11:00 a.m.

Talent Payment: All acts will be paid by company check after the last show on Saturday. Checks may be cashed back through the box office after signing a W-9. This venue will not extend cash advances.

Travel Fees/Arrangements: Travel fees will be paid after the last show on Saturday. Reimbursement for air travel from tickets only. Drivers will be paid a flat $100 unless noted otherwise on the letter of confirmation.

Talent coming by air should call the club with travel plans one week prior to the engagement to schedule ground transfer. If prior arrangements are not made, ground transfer is the responsibility and expense of the act.

Sample format sheet.

for initialing. However, many bookers assume the confirmation responsibility themselves. Some will send a form letter of confirmation outlining the terms of the booking. This is not a binding contract for either side unless it so states. It is a written confirmation of a verbal agreement. Some bookers also send information sheets with the letters of confirmation, giving particulars about the venue. If the booker takes the trouble to write and send these items to you—have the courtesy to read them. The sheets are designed to eliminate questions. Call only about something not covered by any of the information sent.

WHAT IF THE TERMS ARE NOT AGREEABLE?

It may seem sometimes that the comic is always on the short end of the stick, that the booking agents and clubs owners hold all the cards. Not so. The comic can always decline a booking. If a booking is rejected in the appropriate manner and within a reasonable time, there will be no hard feelings from the booker.

What are an appropriate manner and a reasonable time? The best of all possible times to decline a booking is at the time it is offered. At this point no damage has been done to your schedule, the booker's, or the club's. The date offered may be bad for you because of a previous commitment, inconvenient routing, unacceptable pay or slot in the lineup, or any number of reasons. All you need do is decline politely. If the booking agent asks for reasons, be truthful without being rude. Most reputable agents and club owners are business people. They know that not every offer they extend will be accepted. When a comic declines, the booker will either try to renegotiate or withdraw the offer. If you don't know at the point of booking whether or not you can accept the offer, ask for a specific time to think it over. Whatever the time you have asked for, call back promptly with your answer. If the booker gives you the time you have asked for and you do not respond, all bets are off.

If you accept an offer and then cancel after a period of time, you do damage to your relationship with that booker. If you make a habit of accepting offers and then canceling, the word will spread that you are unreliable. Canceling means that the club or the booker must spend more time and effort in covering the hole you left. Depending on the notice you have given, this time investment can be from an hour or so to several days. If a similar comic cannot be found, the show will suffer. Canceling also means more than erasing one name and entering another one. Clubs do publicity work involving pictures and press releases as much as two months in advance. It is impossible for them to change a name in their lineup once the publication has gone to press. This means that perhaps half of their paid advertising, including in some cases their program, will be inaccurate. Any change in the lineup requires that someone from the staff call and sometimes hand-deliver new copy and pictures. The press can be equally put out when changes occur. Like the comic who cancels frequently, the club with constant changes wears out its welcome with local publications.

The person who fares the worst, however, from a job accepted and then rejected is you, the comic. You appear amateurish and unprofessional to the booker. Your behavior will definitely affect your future relationship. Since you have a choice, think what effect accepting or declining this job will have on your career, and make your decision wisely.

13

Confirmations and Cancellations

Comedy is like the weather—it's always changing. It is the wise comedian who takes time to confirm bookings before investing in airplane tickets or arranging for time off from a job. As discussed in Chapter 11, some bookers send a letter of confirmation and an information sheet to the comedian. Bookers who do this can be counted on to write to you (or call, if necessary) about rooms that have folded after you have been booked. To be safe, however, contact the booker about three weeks before the engagement to ask if everything is still OK. If you are telephoning, be sure to confirm with the person who gave you the job. Secretaries, receptionists, and phone people may not have access to the information. Also, if another comedian has a name similar to yours, it would be easy for an assistant to give you inaccurate information. Always go to the source.

If you wish, you may create your own letter of confirmation to mail to the booker. This letter should be short, to the point, and include all pertinent information about the engagement. Set it up so that all the booker has to do is check the dates and numbers, initial the document, and return it to you. Be sure to send a self-addressed, stamped envelope for the return. (You can save money by designing your return on a postcard.) If you do not want to write a form, the Professional Comedians Association has one for member use.

TALENT CANCELLATIONS

When the cancellation comes from you, think through what you are about to do before you take yourself out of a job. Make sure your reason is an absolute emergency. An absolute emergency is a real, documentable medical problem; a real, documentable-on-the-10-o'clock-news weather problem; a real, documentable mechanical problem with your car. When emergencies like those crop up, and they do, call the club and speak with the owner or manager. Explain your circumstances and ask advice in deciding whether to try to make the show. For example, if it is a weather problem, chances are the weather is bad at the club city and the show will be canceled anyway. Do not leave word that you can't make the show with a receptionist, or another comic. It is not their responsibility to do your business. Do not wait until the day after to call and explain why you didn't show. The damage will be greater if you wait.

If you have accepted a future booking and find that you can't honor it, give the club owner as much notice as possible. No matter how you slice it, rebooking is a nuisance. Suggest a few replacements, but check the availability of your fellow comics before you mention their names.

Don't cancel a job because someone offered you $15 more per show in another town. Bookers know what other bookers pay their talent. If one finds that his job has been canceled because another has offered a couple of bucks more, the first booker may not make future offers. Granted, many comics need all the money they

127

can get, but the little extra will not be enough to cover the loss of a booker and all the rooms he or she controls. If you have made a commitment for a dollar amount, honor it.

On the other hand, if the offer is for significantly more money or is a significant career move, the circumstances change. When the "Tonight" show people call, you need to go. When you have this kind of opportunity, call the booker and explain. Most reputable bookers will release you from your obligation and wish you well. That is not to say that you would turn down the "Tonight" show if the booker held you to your date; you wouldn't. But it is good manners to notify the booker. You will be expected to make up the date at a later time for the same money. Should you become a hot talent, your appearance will be a goose for a club that previously could not afford a comic with a "Tonight" show credit. It is only fair that you return one time for the original price. Remember, it is the small clubs and bookers who give young comics a start.

Reputation is everything in this business. If bookers and club owners start to hear that you cancel frequently or fail to show up for jobs, you may be out of a career before you have one.

CLUB CANCELLATIONS

There are four common causes of club cancellation. The club may close. It may rearrange its performance schedule. It may fire a booker and hire one who will not honor previous bookings. It may suffer an act of God (blizzard, hurricane, fire).

When one or more of the above hit you, and they will, there are a few realities to face upon hearing the news. First, getting angry will do you no good, and taking that anger out on the person who calls you with the news is totally inappropriate. Don't shoot the messenger. If you feel that the cancellation is unjust, speak to the person who made the booking.

Do not expect reimbursement for lost wages or travel fees. In most cases, if a show has been canceled, the booker has lost money too.

If the booker cancels you on one show but confirms other bookings, you may assume that the cancellation is through no fault of yours. If, however, a booker pulls all contracted work, take pause. It means that something has gone wrong, personally, between you and the booker or the club. Try to sort out the problem as diplomatically as possible. Perhaps a bad experience with another club has made the booker reluctant to honor your bookings. Perhaps reputation is catching up with you. Whatever the cause, do what you can to gain a second chance. Offer to cut your fee or go in on a lower spot in the lineup to prove your ability. If this doesn't work, ask directly what the problem is. If they tell you, set about righting things as soon as you can.

These cancellations, called "fall outs," are a very real part of this risky business. To protect yourself against these holes in your schedule and the associated financial instability, maintain that savings account. Keep setting aside bits and pieces of paychecks to cover rainy days.

INTERNAL BOOKING CHANGES

The most common internal changes are adding or subtracting shows and the associated income, changes in travel or lodging arrangements, and changes in the status of the performer.

If the club asks you to do more shows than originally scheduled, additional compensation is due. The usual rule is to prorate your shows. Divide your total pay by the original number of shows contracted to get your per-show payment. Multiply that figure by the number of extra shows requested. Then add the product to the contracted fee to get your new talent payment. If shows are subtracted from your contract, do the same process and subtract the result from the contract fee.

Changes in travel or lodging arrangements always come from the club side of the contract. Sometimes the club switches travel agents or hotels. Sometime the budgets for these perks are changed. It is not unusual for a club to change lodging venues, switching hotels or changing from hotel to condo. However, it is a sign of a financially unhealthy club if travel fees are suddenly eliminated.

A change in the status of the performer means one of two things: Your position in the lineup has changed, or your booking status has changed. If your position in the lineup has changed, you will be moved either up or down. If it's up, congratulations, and you should be offered more money. If it's down, proceed with caution. Find out the reason for the demotion, and if it is not acceptable to you, cancel the engagement. A change in booking status means that you or the club has moved. Clubs rarely move, so this is not likely to be a problem. Comics move all the time, and this can be a problem. Fee scales and benefits proposed and accepted at the point of booking prevail. Even if your living circumstances change, the contracted terms are firm. Suppose you are living in Chicago and accept several weeks of work in and around the Chicago area. Then you move to Dallas. It is a given that you are still responsible for filling the Chicago dates. It is also a given that no additional travel or lodging money will be offered because you moved.

If you have moved or changed your name or phone number, it is your responsibility to inform the booker or club owner. If you add articles, special shows, or credits to your press kit, send these to the booker/club owner as soon as you can. Publicity about you in other cities

Eddie Murphy performs his stand-up comedy act for the first time on television in "Eddie Murphy—Delirious," debuting on HBO.

makes you more notable in the booker's city. The more publicity, the easier you are to promote. In fact, all your printed materials (except pictures) should be updated every six to eight months. Even if your credits remain slim, rearranging them may give the appearance of a comic on an upward spiral.

14

Making the Most of Bookings

When bookings are made, all parties hope they will be successful. The club owners want the audience to have a good time and return to spend more money. The bookers want to put together good shows to keep their clients and increase their reputation. The comics want to increase their value to the club and further their career. But how do you, the comic, do it—this increasing your value stuff?

Public relations is the best way to make present and future bookings with a club valuable. Lots of publicity increases the odds that the public will come to see you. More business for the club means more money. If you make more money for the club, you become more valuable. If you are valuable to the club, your bookings will increase. If, on the other hand, your week did poorly and the club made average or less money, you are not valuable to the club. Simple as that. A comic who is not a draw or a potential draw is not a good candidate for another booking. Clubs will overlook a slow week due to Christmas or a special local event, but comics who just put in the time are one- or maybe two-time bookings. Audiences should remember your act, your name, or both when they leave the room.

How is this accomplished? Publicity. How do you get publicity? Two ways: through a public relations person working for the club, or on your own. As soon as you are booked, find out if the club has a publicity/marketing person on staff. About two months before your date, call the PR person and ask what you can do to assist promotion of your week. If the person seems receptive, suggest ideas that have been successful in other clubs. Give specific examples, and offer to help implement them. Let the PR person know you are willing to do some of the drudge work: make phone calls, stuff envelopes. Make it a cooperative effort with the staffer. You will earn points with the club, the staff, and the community.

If the club does not have a public relations person, ask the club owner or booker for permission to pursue some ideas on your own. If you receive permission to do something, follow through, but don't ask for extra money for doing it. The time you spend cultivating your name in a community is an investment in your future as well as the club's. You can, however, ask to use club office equipment (copier, typewriter, FAX, etc.) for your project. Cost of items such as paper and postage can be worked out in advance. At the very worst, offer to split costs with the club.

Many publicity ideas, however, are without cost or relatively inexpensive to implement. You can contact the local newspaper and try to get an article about you printed the weekend before you are to perform. This is a little more involved than just asking for it. You need to come up with an angle or "hook" that makes you interesting. Focus on something unique about yourself or your act. Being a comic is interesting, but a comic who also has a PhD in psychology is better. You may be

Comedienne Rita Rudner.

very funny, but if you are also a world-class bull rider, you have a story. Maybe you left the CIA to be a comic; or you are the tallest comic in the world. Whatever your particular skill or credit, package it in a short press release and send it to the features or entertainment department of the daily newspaper. Follow up with a phone call. Offer to interview over the phone if a personal meeting is geographically difficult.

If you have a favorite charity, offer to do a free performance—then notify the media. The charity sells the tickets, and you get free press on your engagement. Everyone wins.

Offer to do radio interviews and provide some interesting angles. Try for drive-time interviews, preferably morning. Offer to come in a day early, if you can, and help with promotional campaigns. If you can't come in early, be available for phone patch interviews.

Offer to help pass out flyers or tickets for the club. Offer to do teaser shows at luncheons to promote the room. After the show, mingle with the audience or stand at the door as they are exiting and shake hands. Make the audience feel appreciated.

The bottom line in this business is self-promotion. If you just show up, do your set, and leave, you may not have this venue to return to in six months. If you can't think of anything to do to promote your engagement, ask the club owner for suggestions. Try. The club owner is concerned with how well you are going to do for him or her. If you bring in the audience, you have a good shot at return bookings and a raise. Raises are not automatic in this business. They are given to comics who have increased revenue for the club. If you are having a hard time convincing a club owner that you can increase revenue and that you need a raise, offer to share the risk. Offer to come in at a lower-than-normal guaranteed rate vs. a percentage of the box

136

office, whichever is greater. If the club agrees to the deal, get out there and market yourself like crazy. If you pull business into the club, you'll probably make more than on a guaranteed raise, and the club will definitely be happy. Remember, you have a direct effect on what is probably the only source of income for both the club owner and the booker.

AN INTERVIEW WITH RON CRICK

When you watch most comics perform, it's easy to imagine them doing something else. A large part of the comic population looks like they could fit right in as a State Farm salesman or a coach or that guy in personnel. A small percentage of said population doesn't—look that way. There are a very few comics who look and are only that, comics. They are comics because they can't, won't, couldn't be anything else. Even if they had the skills and inclination to be something else, they would still be performers, still be comics. Robin Williams is that way, and so is Bill Hicks and Emo Phillips, and so is Ron Crick.

When you meet him, a first thought is that Ron Crick is a great big guy. An I-beam. A tank. A Big 'n Tall Shop fantasy customer. He has a mop of gray hair, a penchant for loud Hawaiian shirts, and big-as-a-mitt calloused hands. The calluses come from close to thirty years of playing the guitar. Ron Crick is a comic-musician. He has played close to every comedy club in the contiguous US, most as a headline comedian. From Carnegie Hall to a biker bar in Lubbock, Texas, Ron has been there. His résumé has a section that reads "RON CRICK: Where he's been and who he's been with." Then there's a list of people he's worked with in concert, a who's who in music and comedy: Roy Orbison, Billy Crystal, Riders in the Sky, Crystal Gayle, Robert Klein. When they talk about "road warrior"

RON CRICK

comedians and "kings of the road," they are talking about Ron Crick.

Q: When did you first start doing comedy?

A: I started doing comedy before I admitted I was doing comedy. I'd loved music and performing. From being little, I remember listening to music and seeing myself inside it. When I went away to college, I worked in a local band that played for campus stuff. Small stuff. I just got into this habit of talking, making people laugh, playing a little, then making people laugh. It felt comfortable, so I did it. I sort of knew I was funny, and the more I talked to the crowd, the more I got into it. Actually, I never really did just music. Plus it was a way of combatting nerves. If my fingers got nervous (notice I'm saying my fingers were nervous, not me), the talk would loosen me up. Then about '79–'80 I showed up at The [Comix] Annex and started doing comedy there. That was really my first comedy club, although I'd played in tons of nightclubs all over the country by that point.

Q: You mentioned college. Where did you go? Did you graduate? Tell us about it.

A: I went to William Jewell University in Liberty, Missouri. I did graduate. Class of '69 in Sociology. I changed my major a lot—from Physical Education to English to, finally, Sociology. Actually I majored in staying in school and minored in staying out of the draft. It was 1969. Turned out I didn't pass the physical to go into the Army, so I wouldn't have gone [to Viet Nam] anyway. In college I had this band and we would hang out with Shake Russell and

Dana Cooper and play. So while I was figuring out what I wanted to do, I was doing it.

Q: Did you ever consider pursuing only music? Being a serious songwriter?

A: I *am* a serious song writer. I write music with the same approach that I do comedy. One of my songs has been recorded and written up in *Billboard* as a "pick of the week." It was called "Hello, This Is Anna." I wrote it with Nate Herman from Second City*. OB McClinton recorded it on the Epic label. Made a couple of bucks from it.

Q: How would you define your musical style?

A: Kind of irreverent country. Someone influenced by Asleep at the Wheel or Commander Cody.

Q: What was your worst night in comedy, so far?

A: There were two of them. First was Lubbock. There was this biker bar that decided to hire comics. So the agent calls and I go and everyone is bombed. They see me and my guitar, and they start yelling for me to play some Jimmy Buffet. They didn't want to hear jokes. So I'm doing the parts of my act that I think they can understand. I'm half way through when the manager *pages* someone over the PA. I'm in shock—this is the manager! But I get past it. Then he does it again—and then a third time. After the third time I walked. Left the stage.

The second worst night was in New York. I

---

* The legendary improvisational revue theater in Chicago. Better known for quick-witted actors than stand-up comics, Second City produced talent like John Belushi, Gilda Radner, John Candy, Bill Murray, and Dan Ackroyd. Many alumni have gone on to stardom on "Saturday Night Live."

was just starting out performing professionally. I was at this club called The Other End. It was owned by the people who had The Bitter End. Anyway it was July 4 weekend, and I was opening for George Thorogood. First night went great. It was opening night and they had champagne and flowers, and *Variety* was there to review us. I got interviewed. Everything was great. Second night was death. I was terrible. The crowd was terrible. If I'd known more, my feelings hurt would have been hurt. I stayed on stage just to punish the audience. Afterward the owner, Paul Colby, comes up to me and says, "That's the worst show I ever saw." I say, "Well, Paul, this is the perfect room for it." He just laughed and said, "You got me, Crickster."

Q: What was the best night in comedy, so far?

A: Carnegie Hall. I was opening for Don McLean in Houston in August of '84. He liked my stuff, and we hit it off pretty well. Out of the blue he asks me if I want to open for him in November in New York. Didn't say the name of the hall or anything. I say OK. When I found out we were playing Carnegie Hall, I told him "I don't know what you're paying me, but I need 34 comps." That November I had Thanksgiving dinner at home in New Jersey, and the next night my whole family got to see me perform at Carnegie Hall.

Q: How do you get your material?

A: Over the years I've gotten more academic about writing. I actually sit down and write stuff from time to time. Mostly I trip over material. I'm out and about and I see something that might work. Accidents happen on stage that might turn into something. An ad lib in a show could produce a new bit. Something leads to something leads to something. What I do religiously is read the newspapers. When I'm on the road I read two or three papers a day and I watch TV news, CNN. I'm always looking for a new bit. I use a lot of topical material, stuff based on current events. So I have to keep changing my stuff to be up-to-date.

Q: Has anyone ever stolen any of your material?

A: Sure. Once while I was working with them. I was headlining in a room in South Carolina and on the second night [of a week] the woman feature went up and did my opening bit. When she came off stage I was standing there, and she looks at me real sheepish and says I might want to change my opening. She had just done it, sorry very much. The rotten thing was that she stole the material and I got punished. I had to watch her act for the rest of the week to make sure she didn't steal anything more—and she was terrible.

Q: What advice would you give young people starting out in comedy?

A: Don't be in a hurry. Take the time you need to train and get good. Sell guitars or something until you're really good, not just ready. Too many eager beavers think the minute they get twenty minutes they should quit job, school, fill in the blank, and hit the road. Wait. Instead of watching an amateur night and thinking "I can do better than that," watch pros, someone good, and try to be better than that. Ultimately the eager beavers will kill the market. They aren't ready for an audience, but they work dirt-cheap so people hire them. They do a lousy

Comedian and actor Robin Williams shares a laugh with singer James Taylor while filming promotional spots for an upcoming "Saturday Night Live."

job, people won't come back to the club, and the club goes out of business. The end result is the club owner thinks comedy won't work, audiences think comedy won't work, and the real comics are out of work. Take it easy. If you're really good, things will happen.

Q: What is "making it" for you?

A: I used to think it was money and fame. 'Course, you can always make more money. But I really think it's being able to do what you want to do and pay the bills. Too many people get trapped in jobs—they lose their dreams, their careers. I would like to earn the respect of my peers and be able to live and be a comic.

15

The "Them-Us" Relationship

Because the comedy field is still fairly young and the businesses tend to be small, it's easy for the classic "them-us" relationship to arise between the club owner or booker and the comic. The "them-us" relationship assumes that all club owners are greedy money grubbers and all comics are tortured artists, or club owners are selfless keepers of the art and comics are spoiled and egotistical. The truth of the matter is that each side has difficult job-related problems that sometimes are not realized or considered by the other side. When one side begins to appreciate the other, the clubs and the artists realize once again that the show doesn't go on without the business and vice versa.

Let's review the matter from the comedian's point of view. Before any money starts to come in, the comic has invested a great deal of time, energy, and personal finances. There was the time spent as an amateur and all the rejections associated with this period. Money has been spent on marketing materials that may never be recovered. On an already small income, the comic may have had to spend money on travel and sometimes lodging *before* the engagement pays. There was more

145

rejection and frustration trying to get those first few bookings. There is the self-promotion necessary just to keep afloat. Comics live in a constant state of flux. They travel all the time, juggling family, bookings, school, and extra jobs just to go up somewhere. Once a comic starts making money, it is impossible to predict what a yearly or monthly income will be. Clubs close, weather prevents shows, bookings are mixed up, and budgets are tightened. The comic works in a crowded arena but spends most of the time alone. Short engagements don't leave much time to build meaningful relationships. Once on the road, the comic must adjust to new living arrangements literally every week; this is disorienting and gives one a sense of having no roots. The isolation and lifestyle in general make the comic an easy mark for depression and substance abuse. The comic must be his or her own cheerleader, motivator, and nurturer. This is all difficult to do and stay sane. The drive to succeed in show business must be overpowering to keep going in the face of so many negatives. It's no wonder that comics hate to leave a stage when people are laughing and clapping. The instant gratification is necessary grease to the wheel of a comedy career. A career in comedy takes not only talent but guts and courage.

The other side of the coin is the comedy club owner. Whereas as the comic is constantly on the move, the club owner is tied hand and foot to that club. The person interested in club ownership immediately makes a substantial financial investment, which requires hands-on management and savvy business sense to succeed. It is unlikely that a person who wants to own a comedy club will go through the pains of building a facility only to drop it into the hands of an unsupervised manager. The owner, even if he or she owns several clubs, must be a presence felt by the staff and the talent. This takes time and effort. Let's look at the areas of expenditure required of the club owner before the first customer is served: lease or purchase of a property; remodeling or renovation of the property; purchase of furniture, bar supplies, office equipment, sound and lighting equipment—any physical thing inside or outside the club that needs to be maintained, fixed, or supplied; licenses and insurance policies; taxes, payroll, promotional expenses, and services like cleaning, accounting, security, and lodging. Even with minimum dollar figures attached to each item, the initial investment for the club owner is in the hundreds of thousands of dollars.

Once the club is open and audiences materialize, the club owner may look like a fat cat trying to squeeze a seemingly underpaid and poorly appreciated artist. The comic sees a nightclub full of laughing, drinking people who have paid a cover charge. The comic sees his or her talent fee and realizes that it is only a small percentage of what must be walking through the door. It becomes easy for the comic to build resentment about what seems an inequitable distribution of wealth. It becomes easy for the comic to see the club owner as an insensitive person with a closed mind.

What the comic may not see is this: A full house does not mean that every person has paid a full cover charge. Clubs offer group discounts to businesses, free passes to nonprofit organizations, and half-price tickets to the general public as an incentive. Weekends tend to have more full-price ticket buyers, but weeknights, in full-week rooms, are used to attract customers looking for bargains.

But bars make lots of money, you say. Doesn't the club owner rake it in at the bar? A bar may be busy but, again, all is not pure profit. Before a bar can open, it needs a license and expensive equipment. Before a bar starts counting profit, it must first pay a monthly state tax (in most states) equivalent to 10 to 15 percent of gross sales. Usually this fee is due by the fifteenth of the month in cash; failure to comply means closure before the month is over. While most bars do make a profit, they are also expensive to run and often need repairs, replacements, or renewals, leaving the owner cash-poor.

If attendance is light for any reason, it is the owner who feels the crunch in the pocketbook. The owner's financial responsibilities do not lessen with a poor week. The last person to realize money from a comedy club is the owner.

So while the comic is struggling, the owner is too. Comics and club owners who learn to respect the job the other is doing will prosper. For the comic to expect the club owner to make his world a better place is as unrealistic as for the club owner to expect one comic to turn his business into a success. Comedy clubs thrive if there are professionals on both sides of the lights.

16

General Dos and Don'ts In Comedy

Let's assume at this point that you: (a) have made a conscious decision to be a professional stand-up comedian, (b) have done all the preliminary marketing and amateur work, (c) have worked your way up through the ranks, and (d) have gotten a chance to work at jobs that will take you on the road to a bright new career. Don't blow it at this point. Don't think that the battle is over and you are on the yellow brick road to stardom. Keep your wits about you and take heed of the following:

Always arrive on time for a job. Your call time, or time when you are expected to check in at the club, is something you should know from the time of booking. There is no excuse for arriving late for an engagement short of an act of God. Telling the club owner you got lost, misplaced your map, or ran out of gas is like telling a teacher the dog ate your homework (and about as believable). If you are unsure of travel time, leave early. If you need directions, call the club in advance. If an act of God has occurred, call the club and report to the *person in charge*. Some clubs consider lateness as grounds for firing on the spot. A comic who is late and has to be replaced will not get paid.

Always dress well. Unless a costume is part of your act, clean and pressed is the order of the day. No one expects you to walk on stage with a million-dollar wardrobe. You are expected to wear clothing that fits you and moves comfortably on stage. Some comics keep one or two street outfits for stage work. Sloppy T-shirts, dirty sneakers, and greasy hair are totally unacceptable. Carry a small travel iron with you and press your clothing before you appear on stage.

Always clear technical needs in advance. If your act uses audiotapes, videotapes, or light changes, find out at the point of booking who is the technical person at the club and meet with that person before the house opens for the first show. It's a good idea to be self-contained as a comic, but audio or visual aids can add variety to an act. If you use them, take responsibility for them. Cue your tapes before each show, communicate exact cue lines for the technician, set and check your own props, and tune your instrument before you hit the stage. Accidents and bloopers are bound to happen, but you can eliminate many bugs by thorough preshow checks and regular maintenance of your equipment.

Party with caution at the club. The comedy club is your workplace and should be treated as such. Even though people like to buy drinks for the entertainer, even though everyone in the club is partying, you are being paid for your work there. Stay away from alcohol before you do your show. Alcohol will not make you funnier, smarter, faster, better looking, or more confident. Talent and a good act will do all of the above; alcohol only gives the illusion. If you must drink, do so after the whole show is over, and in moderation. If audience members or fellow comics want to buy you a drink, tell the bartender to send you a soda. A comedy

150

club bartender will be glad to make it look like a mixed drink by adding fruit, and no one will be the wiser.

Being drunk on stage is grounds for dismissal without pay, show or no show. Club owners do not want the liability of a performer who leaves his or her bar drunk.

All of the above also applies to drugs. Drugs are illegal. Buying, selling, or using drugs in the club puts the entire operation in jeopardy. The club could lose its liquor license or occupancy permit if illegal drugs are bought, sold, or used on the premises.

Life on the road is hard, and it may seem as if alcohol or drugs can "take the edge off." Not true. If you cannot perform without a drink or a drug, seek professional help. Alcoholics Anonymous has meetings everywhere; you need never be far from a good support group. Call the local number. Someone will give you meeting times, directions, and even pick you up for meetings if necessary.

Learn to handle details without going off the deep end. Each comedy booking will be a little bit the same and a little bit different. Ask what you need to know to get you to the right place at the right time. Use plain old common sense when calling for information. Calling an agent in Houston to say that you have arrived at the Chicago airport is pointless; call the club in Chicago and tell them you have arrived. Think through where you need to be and when you need to be there, and make plans accordingly. Trouble happens, so allow time for it.

Don't whine! Club owners, booking agents, and club staffs are as different as snowflakes. Comics are treated a little bit the same and a little bit different in every club. It is pointless to complain to a club owner that you are not being treated as well as you are in other clubs. If you find that you don't like a club, for whatever reason, don't book back. Be polite, do your show, thank everyone, and then get the hell out of Dodge. No one forced you to take the booking. No one will force you to return.

Some situations, however, create legitimate cause to talk to the management. It is reasonable to do so if some aspect of the engagement is hazardous. Perhaps you have been lodged in a condo and the front-door lock is broken. A request for repair is reasonable. If someone from the audience or another comic becomes abusive, request that the management deal with the offender. If some aspect of the engagement is contrary to your written agreement, talk to management and work things out before you do another show. If your request is reasonable, it is likely that the problem will be solved quickly.

The time to be pushy and aggressive is in promoting your act. Put all your energy into making a splash on stage, and take care of your personal needs privately. Wasting time hustling a club owner for a free drink is rude. Good manners are appreciated and remembered.

Complimentary tickets or beverages. Find out in advance the club's policy on complimentary tickets and drinks. Keep this policy in mind when you order at the bar or invite friends to see your show.

Whatever the policy on complimentary tickets, it is good manners to invite guests on nights that are normally not well attended, which usually means weeknights. If it is impossible for your guests to come on a slow night, suggest that they pay for weekend tickets or buy the tickets for them. If the club offers you complimentary tickets, be sure to tell the reservation person exactly how many and for when. If a guest cancels, have the courtesy to notify the reservation desk.

As a rule, clubs offer comics unlimited complimentary tickets unless the seat can be sold. If a guest is in a seat that can be sold, the guest can purchase the seat, the comic can purchase the seat, or the guest can leave and come back during a less crowded performance. It is also appropriate to tell your guests to order a beverage from the bar. It need not be alcoholic, but the guest should make some small contribution to the club.

Find out the club policy for complimentary beverages before you order from the bar. Some clubs allow comedians unlimited drinks after their show. Some clubs allow one or two free drinks and charge for subsequent beverages. Still other clubs allow unlimited coffee and soda and charge a discounted price for other drinks. Whatever the club policy, it applies only to you, not your spouse, your date, or your friends.

Cashing your paycheck. An ongoing dilemma for the stand-up comedian is dealing with the paycheck. Most clubs pay their talent by company check. Most road comics do not live in the cities where they play. What to do with this out-of-town or out-of-state check?

Find out the policy when you arrive at the club. Most clubs allow the artist to cash the check at the bar or box office. This makes things easy, although it does leave you with the problem of carrying around large amounts of cash. However, some venues do not cash checks either for employees or for artists. In such case the comic has several options (that don't involve whining). The comic can ask to be paid before the last show and cash the check at the venue's bank. The comic can stay in town long enough to cash the check at the venue bank after the engagement is over. The comic can keep an account with a national bank chain. The national bank chain is the best option; it allows you to make deposits and withdrawals wherever you are working. It is unsafe to travel with large amounts of cash, but if you choose to handle your money this way, be sure you have some provisions for security.

Budget your money and avoid asking for cash ad-

153

vances. Since you know your schedule, you should know about how much cash you will need until your next paycheck. Comics who get to an engagement with two dimes in their pocket and immediately ask for a cash advance diminish their appearance immediately. Many venues, especially ones in hotels, do not issue cash advances to employees. If you are flat broke in such a club, you could be in serious trouble. Maintain a credit card or keep enough cash in pocket to see you through the engagement. Be considerate. Wait for the designated time to be paid.

In Closing

Congratulations! You have finished this book and should now have the information you need to decide once and for all if stand-up comedy is the career for you. If you take another look in the mirror and say, "Sure, I can handle everything mentioned and then some," go for it! Comedy is a wonderful career. If, on the other hand, some things about the life-style bother you, find another career. There is no fiction in the book. Everything is based on firsthand knowledge by a writer who knows the business.

Comedy as a craft will always change. Shows evolve. The comics who kept 'em laughing in the burlesque halls probably wouldn't get a giggle from today's audiences. The business end, however, has changed very little. You will not be able to embrace the performing part of comedy without also embracing the business end. And the business end will not change just because you don't agree with it. Show business is two words: You can't succeed at one without taking care of the other. The comedy clubs can't exist without the comics, and the comics can't work without the clubs. (If you doubt this, ask some of the comics who have been

An ecstatic Tracey Ullman celebrates her 1989 Emmy award for outstanding variety, music, or comedy program for "The Tracey Ullman Show."

working for a while. They'll tell you how difficult it was to find a stage, much less get paid to perform.)

The first booking in a club is easy, but it takes a professional stand-up comedian to get the return engagement. Good luck to you all, and that's a wrap!

Glossary

The following terms are comedy industry jargon or slang used in this book. Some terms may be used in other aspects of the entertainment world; the definitions below pertain only to the comedy industry.

bio or biography A one–page statement of personal information.

bit A specific piece of material in a routine. "He did well with the restaurant *bit*."

call time Time designated for the comedian to arrive at the club and check in with the person in charge; usually an hour to half an hour before showtime.

drop list List of performers who may no longer sign up for amateur night or workout-night slots.

fall out Used by comedians, a booking that was canceled, for whatever reason. Used by booking agents, a slot that was booked but canceled by the comedian. Comedians ask bookers to call them if they should have any fall outs, or sudden, unexpected cancellations.

gig An isolated paying job. "I had a *gig* in Toledo."

go up The physical act of going onto the stage to perform. "What time do I *go up*?"

greenroom Communal room where performers can wait before, after, and between times on stage.

headshot Photograph of a person from the middle of the neck up.

"I killed!" Remark made by a stand-up comedian who

thinks he or she has just had an extremely successful show. "Man, I killed in Houston!"

off night 1. Night when the club is not open; also called *dark night*. 2. Night when a comedian thinks he or she did poorly. "Boy, I really had an off night last night."

professional (pro) 1. A person who is paid for specific services in a field also worked by amateurs. 2. A comedian with a great deal of experience in adapting to a variety of performing circumstances.

road Term denoting any work outside the home city. "I'm going on the road tomorrow."

session Set time spent shooting publicity pictures, recording radio commercials, or filming features, commercials, industrial film, or cable projects. Base fees for services are usually calculated according to the number of sessions involved.

set Collective term for the total time the comedian is on stage during a particular show.

showcase Live, unpaid audition in front of an audience and the club booking agent.

venue Actual, physical performance room.

For Further Reading

Bruce, Lenny. *How to Talk Dirty and Influence People*. Englewood Cliffs, NJ: Simon & Schuster, 1965.

Buzzell, Linda. *How to Make It in Hollywood*. New York: HarperCollins, 1992.

Carter, Joseph. *Never Met a Man I Didn't Like: The Life and Writing of Will Rogers*. New York: Avon Books, 1991.

Chandler, Charlotte. *Hello, I Must be Going . . . Groucho and His Friends*. New York: Carol Publishing Group, 1992.

Collier, Denise, and Beckett, Kathleen. *Spare Ribs: Women in the Humor Biz*. New York: St. Martin's Press, 1980.

Corey, Melinda, and Ochoa, George. *Movies and TV: The New York Public Library Book of Answers*. Englewood Cliffs, NJ: Simon & Schuster, 1992.

Goldman, Albert. *Ladies and Gentlemen . . . Lenny Bruce*. New York: Penguin Books, 1992.

Henry, William A. *The Great One: The Life and Legend of Jackie Gleason*. New York: Doubleday, 1992.

Hill, Doug, and Weingrad, Jeff. *Saturday Night*. New York: Vintage Books, 1987.

Logan, Tom. *Acting in the Million Dollar Minute*. New York: Broadcasting Publication, Inc, 1984.

Marx, Harpo, with Barber, Rowland. *Harpo Speaks*. New York: Limelight Editions, 1985.

Quinlan, David. *Quinlan's Illustrated Directory of Comedy Actors*. New York: Henry Holt & Co., 1992.

Rivers, Joan, and Meryman, Richard. *Still Talking*. New York: Avon Books, 1991.

Spolin, Viola. *Improvisation for Theatre*. Evanston, IL: Northwestern University Press, 1983.

Index

161